CW00347608

Dancing
on
Eggshells

Dancing on Eggshells

JOHN WHAITE

K

An Hachette UK Company
www.hachette.co.uk

First published in Great Britain in 2023 by
Kyle Books, an imprint of Octopus Publishing Group Limited
Carmelite House
50 Victoria Embankment
London EC4Y 0DZ
www.octopusbooks.co.uk

ISBN: 9781804191491

Distributed in the US by Hachette Book Group, 1290 Avenue of the Americas,
4th and 5th Floors, New York, NY 10104

Distributed in Canada by Canadian Manda Group,
664 Annette St., Toronto, Ontario, Canada M6S 2C8

Publishing Director: Judith Hannam
Publisher: Joanna Copestick
Editor: Tara O'Sullivan
Editorial Assistant: Emma Hanson
Jacket Design: Mel Four
Production: Emily Noto

Printed and bound in Great Britain

10 9 8 7 6 5 4 3 2 1

This FSC® label means that materials used for the product
have been responsibly sourced

To Paul – my Northern Star.
And in loving memory of Basil.

Contents

Foreword

BY STEPH MCGOVERN

I am writing this while eating one of John's coconut macaroon brownies (I say one, I'm on my third now). Despite the voice in my head saying 'just have a bite, don't eat the lot', I can't stop myself. That's the thing with John – you have one little nibble of what he has to offer and you just want to devour the lot. No euphemism intended (that's a lie, most of our conversations are filthy).

John, who is of course a *GBBO* champion, made the brownies for me on the TV show we work on together (*Steph's Packed Lunch*, Channel 4) and the more I think about it, the more I realise that these little squares of coconutty, meringuey, chocolately deliciousness are pretty much John in cake form. Yes, gorgeous, that's obvious. Half the nation fancies John Whaite but I think that's the least interesting thing about him. John, like his brownies, is rich in layers . . . the fluffy and playful top ones followed by the deeper ones full of flavour and complexity. And much like the coconut in this particular recipe, there's a sprinkling of randomness too. Together they make one hell of a bloke that I feel very lucky to have in my life.

We first met about three years ago when I was putting together what we call the 'family' for my TV show. I never take any notice of cooking programmes so I had no idea who he was, but that didn't matter. The minute he walked into the room I loved him. His Wigan wit, his forensic mind, his gentle nature, his naughtiness coupled with the unusual career path he had carved for himself made him a joy to chat to. And we haven't stopped chatting since.

John is also one of the cleverest people I know. Whether we're debating the obesity crisis, toxic masculinity, artificial intelligence or whether inspirational quotes on cushions are naff, John brings the chats to life. He listens to other views, takes time to learn the facts, which he sometimes carries around on scraps of paper, and isn't afraid to stand up for what he believes in. He is someone you want to be around. Your clever mate who you like going out with because you'll have a laugh and learn stuff from too.

You will also never find a man more honest than John. Some might say too honest. I have been known to turn up in his dressing room moments before we are about to go on air to check that he really wants to say what I know he is about to reveal on telly. His response is always the same. 'It's me, though, isn't it. If I'm going to be honest, I have to be honest about everything.' This is what you're about to get shed loads of in this book. Raw, uncensored and, at times, uncomfortable truths.

So go on, get comfy and let yourself enter the wonderful and crackers world of John Robert Whaite . . . enjoy.

Coconut Macaroon Brownies

Seeing as Steph mentioned these brownies, I thought it best to include them, just in case the very mention of them got your heart racing. They're a chewy, dense brownie, topped with a light coconut macaroon meringue mixture. They're definitely intense and layered, just like yours truly (according to Ms McGovern).

For the brownie batter
135g (4⅔oz) dark chocolate pieces
135g (4⅔oz) unsalted butter, diced
175g (6oz) caster sugar
100g (3½oz) plain flour
2 large eggs
Sea salt flakes

For the topping
2 large egg whites
120g (4 ½oz) caster sugar
120g (4 ½oz) desiccated coconut

- Preheat the oven to 200°C/180°C fan/400°F/gas mark 6. Grease and line a 20cm (8in) square cake tin, preferably loose-bottomed, with baking paper (parchment paper).

- Put the butter and chocolate into a heatproof bowl and set over a pan of simmering water. Stir occasionally until melted and glossy, then remove from the heat – it's always wise to wipe the base of the bowl to prevent any condensation from getting into the mixture. Mix in the sugar, flour and salt until combined, then beat in the eggs. When you first add the eggs, the mixture will look grainy and split, but keep beating and it should become smooth and velvety. Pour into the prepared cake tin and set aside until needed.

- For the coconut topping, whisk the egg whites until foamy, then gradually add the sugar while whisking – I do this on a high speed in my freestanding electric mixer, but it can be done in a bowl with handheld electric whisk. Once the sugar has been added, continue whisking until you have a thick and smooth meringue, then fold in the coconut with a spatula. Spread the macaroon mixture onto the brownie layer and level it out with a small palette knife or the back of a spoon.

- Bake for 30 minutes, then allow to cool completely. Once cooled, refrigerate for at least 2 hours (or freeze for an hour) so you can slice them as neatly as possible – wipe the knife in between cuts with a damp cloth to help cut cleanly.

A Proper Cuppa

———

Before I begin, I want to get something very straight (perhaps not the best line with which to open a memoir that is full of stories about gay shame and struggle, but a little gallows humour never hurt a soul): how to make a cup of tea. I consider myself a fairly liberal chap, open-minded and used to going with the flow. But when it comes to my brew, I am evangelical and devout, unwavering and unquestioning. Admittedly, I didn't get to this stage of brewing bigotry without some trial and error. I've supped many a too-bitter cuppa before now, and have retched a few times at the pale and weak milkiness of a bag-meets-water-for-a-second mug of pond filth. That kind of tea is an abomination to all of humanity.

I'm writing this introduction with a cup of tea made to a very strict protocol – one, I should add, that has changed hundreds of people's opinions on how to make the perfect brew. I have shared this method several times over the past few years on Instagram, and of all the recipes I've effortfully tested, retested, tweaked and shared, this one has had the most feedback.

First, I fill my mug with boiling water to warm it. There's no need to discard the water – that would be wasteful. Instead, I either pour it back into the kettle, or tip it into a second mug to cool and swig later. The teabag goes into the warmed mug. While I'm a proud Lancashire lad, the War of the Roses is expunged from record while I'm making my tea – Yorkshire Tea, for the win. I pour the recently boiled water on to the teabag and set a timer for seven minutes precisely. I cover the mug with a saucer to keep everything wonderfully hot, then, when the time is up, I DO NOT SQUEEZE THE TEABAG. Instead, I gently escort it from cup to bin with a spoon. Squeezing the teabag makes the tea bitter. If my partner makes me a brew in which a squeezed teabag has been involved, I spit it out furiously.

You can keep your teapots and cosies, your loose-leaf teas and your strainers. I like a bag.

Now that's all ironed out, I shall begin.

Preface

———

I never thought I'd write a memoir. I never thought I'd do a lot of the things I have done in my thirty-four years, but life has a wonderful way of surprising us. I've never really liked surprises – I was the child who ransacked the cupboards at Christmas to find the presents, who was insistent on never, ever having a surprise birthday bash. If one could learn to predict the future, I'd be first on the waiting list. But having this opportunity was a gift of fate I couldn't decline.

It's one of the hardest things I've ever had to do. Naturally, it's an emotional drag, but it's difficult in a logistical sense, too. Trying to summon memories after time, tequila and trauma have eroded many of my brain cells has been an irksome task at times. It has taken great discipline, stamina and organisation; traits that, as I get older, seem to be more evasive and as rare as hens' teeth. But I think I got there in the end. One way of coping with this – and something in which I rarely allowed myself to indulge in the past – was submitting and giving up for the day. The process of writing my memoir has taught me that if the day is against you – one of those endless, insurmountable days when every single thing seems to be off balance and discordant – then you should simply accept it's a shit day and do something else. Something enjoyable. You might think that life is too short to give up for the day, but as a friend once corrected me: life is too bloody long *not* to.

It's been quite painful at times – very painful, in fact. To look back on difficult memories, moments when I wish I could just bob back in time and change a particular course of action to prevent myself from making the wrong choices, has been embarrassing, shame-inducing (though I'll come on to that, eventually), tear-jerking and revelatory. Someone like Oprah might call these 'teachable moments': opportunities to learn and grow. Embarrassment, shame, guilt – all the negative emotions and feelings – are gifts to us. I know that sounds so hippy-dippy and platitudinal, but it's the truth. Sugar-coated or raw, the fact is we can learn from our mistakes. We can choose to let them hack us down, fell us like old, infected elms, or we can choose to see them as the mallet and chisel of Michelangelo, sculpting us, making us more polished.

This, I guess, is my story about just that: learning and growing up. I came to fame in 2012, aged twenty-three, through the hit TV show *The Great British Bake Off*. In years, I was a young man, but in my head, I was still very much a child, confused and unsure of his identity and pathway. Over the last ten years, I've had to mature, narrowly scraping through, and deal with the loss of my partner, my home, my life.

Reflecting on one's past *is* growth, and if that's a huge part of therapy, then writing this book has been an intense crash course of a Harley Street standard. I've had multiple rounds of therapy over the years – some good, some terrible – but none of that has compared to sitting here, writing these words, mulling over whether I should reveal my truth to you, a complete stranger. But a huge part of moving forward is accepting the truth, without shame or judgement. Look at the snapshot, look at what you learned, and move forward.

One of the more challenging aspects of growth I have dealt with is the separation from my parents. I live only three miles or so away from them, and I've only recently had that eye-opening revelation that many people experience much younger – and others, sadly, never – that I am *not* my parents. I can disagree with them, while respecting them. I can feel the bitter sting of their hurtful words, while pitying their own strife and pain. I can find their opinions indigestible, while enjoying sharing food and company with them. They are and I am separate, individual masses of atoms, linked solely by blood. Sometimes, you just have to be the firebreak in your family tree and move away from the pack.

It's a hard pill to swallow for so many. We grow up being told never to question the priest, the police, our parents, but our individuality demands otherwise. Finding the right balance between bending these ancient, arcane rules and breaking them is one of the hardest parts of getting older. But when you get through that tricky time, life seems to fall back into place again.

What is true for me may not necessarily be true for others, but I've found that as I've navigated those first hurdles of life – mistakes and separation – empathy has been the trophy. With a sense of context and resolve, growth allows us to more easily consider the perspectives of others as they make mistakes – affecting themselves, another or me – and to forgive them. Forgiveness is a milestone in the journey of love. Without reaching that granite marker, the pathway is closed off for the winter.

Life with other people can be painful and gut-wrenching. The words, actions or absence of others can leave you heavily winded and writhing on the ground in agony. But, I fear, it's all part of the bigger picture. We are here to have our hearts shattered into a million pieces from time to time, so that we can rebuild it.

You might expect food to feature prominently throughout this book, given my rise to fame and subsequent career as a TV chef. Well, there's definitely food in here. At times, I'll give you a handful of recipes in a chapter; at others, there'll be little mention, if any. The truth is, while food has the ability to soothe my soul, it can also chill me to the bone. As someone with bulimia, I can be haunted as much as comforted by food, and that's a war I'm still very much fighting. Food can be concomitant with guilt and shame. It's definitely here, spattered across many of these pages, but its presence is sometimes a little more subtle.

Perhaps it's linked to the bulimia – probably, but I really don't know for sure – but the pain of growing up gay in a world that still wasn't quite ready to accept me as such has certainly shaped me as a man. I still don't think the world *is* yet fully accepting of queer people, but it does fill me with fizzing joy to see the kids of today enjoy their aesthetic fluidity and freedom to roam within their own boundaries of sexuality. That's not to say every young person feels liberated – many are still bullied and persecuted for their sexuality or gender – but I hope my story will offer solace to those souls.

This book can sometimes be a little morbid. I won't apologise for that. I think each day we walk the earth, we skirt a little closer to the end. Surprisingly, that fact – memento mori – has been a remedy to my darker days of depression and alcohol abuse. As Jack 'Dr Death' Kevorkian said: 'When there is nothing left to burn, you have to set yourself on fire.' I've found doing so hasn't left me in a pile of ashes on the floor, but has instead burnished and rejuvenated me, fired away the bullshit and left the glistening embers of truth. And on that note, dear reader, allow me to present you with *my* truth.

1.
Polystyrene Volcanoes and Peeling Potatoes

———

I was conceived above a chip shop. Sorry if that's oversharing, but I always think it an entertaining way to start a conversation when I meet someone for the first time. I don't know the finer details, and I'm not going to interrogate my parents, but the limited – yet unsurprisingly sufficient – span of my knowledge is that at the time, my parents owned the chippy in Clitheroe, Lancashire, and the thing that people traditionally need to do to make a baby was done. My two older sisters, Jane and Victoria, are always curiously happy to let me know that I was an accident, though my mum likes to put a more positive spin on that narrative and refers to me as a 'miracle'. Sibling rivalry can be bitter, and a mother's love too sickly sweet – dark chocolate versus white. To be honest, both sides are a little extreme: I'm neither mistake nor miracle, just another well-arranged scramble of atoms on this marbled bowling ball.

Before I was born, my parents moved about thirty miles south, to a small Lancashire farming village, where they opened yet another chip shop. It was the kind of sleepy village where, as you strolled past the gun shop or wandered by the duck pond, you'd bump into someone you knew and get talking for ages. The friendly sort of place where if you sneezed on the bus, an old lady would offer you her hanky – not like London, where people scowl at you if you so much as breathe near them. In the summertime, the children of the village – me included – would roam the fields and strip to our underwear to splash and cool ourselves in the weir. We weren't tethered to phones back then – this was the 90s; most of us didn't even have watches that weren't the edible kind from a sweet shop. We just knew that when dusk fell, we were to disperse and flee home before our mothers opened the door to shout our names into the twilight.

We were a close, working-class family. Dad was a painter and decorator when he wasn't in the chippy, and Mum was a trainee nurse in my very early years. She'd work nights at the hospital, so I'd snuggle in bed with Dad. In the afternoons I'd sit on his knee and stroke his face for hours as I sat staring at the TV. The prickle of his stubble on my fingertips lulled me into a trance.

When I was in high school, when my own stubble was just about starting to peer through the smoothest parts of the skin on my chin, I would get the bus to the chip shop every afternoon to peel the potatoes, which was my job. I never remembered to take my key, but if the front door's bottom lock wasn't bolted, I could use my bus pass to open the door by slotting it between the latch and the latch bore – like a burglar in a black-and-white film.

It was monotonous work, peeling spuds. The room always had a watery, starchy smell, because the peeled potatoes would sit in great buckets of cold water to keep them from oxidising and turning greyish brown. As I'd start my shift after school, I'd often work in my uniform, and no matter how many times it went through the washing machine, it would always have a faint smell of starch, frying oil and cow poo (by this time, I lived on a dairy farm).

I'd collect the 25-kilogram sacks of spuds from the shed at the back, which, during winter, was bloody freezing. Twenty-five kilograms is nothing now, but I struggled with the sacks back then, often dropping them as I hobbled into the potato room, then dragged them along the floor of red broken tiles. I remember the first time Mum showed me how to open the bags, which were tied with threaded pieces of string; if you cut and pulled the string in a certain way, it would slip out in one go. Normally, I'd get it wrong, then have to go along the string, unpicking it section by section with my flip knife, chasing it as it snaked through the paper, which took ages.

Once the bag of spuds was open, I'd tip some into the rumbler – a huge stainless-steel contraption, shaped a little like a Dalek. I'd take off the black rubber lid and throw the potatoes into the spinning drum, which was lined with a coarse, sandpaper-like material that always made me recoil with a grimace and wince if I accidentally touched it – rather like the reaction I have when I take off my woollen gloves with my teeth, and the material squeaks against the enamel.

The rumbler would rub the skin off the potatoes and clean them at the same time, but if you let it go on for too long, the potatoes would be reduced to slimy pebbles. Sometimes, if they were extra dirty or full of eyes, I'd over-rumble them on purpose, and Mum would go mad at me for wasting perfectly good food. When the rumbling was done, I'd open the hatch on the front of the machine, and the potatoes would come flying out into my yellow bucket, or miss and dart all over the room, sliding across the floor like wet fish. I'd then have to remove the eyes, which I hated. There was something about sticking the tip of the knife into the potato and rotating it with a crackling squeak that made the hairs on my neck stand on end. Sometimes, I'd cheat and just lob great wedges off the spud, and of course I'd get in trouble for that. But when you had endless bucketloads of tatties to get through, it seemed like a sacrifice worth making. The potatoes, eye-free and perfectly peeled, would then go into the huge vats of cold water, ready to be scooped into the chipper.

★ ★ ★

My earliest memory of the chippy, though, is of me sitting on the salt-speckled counter dressed as Peter Pan: green tights, a little green smock cinched with a belt and a felt hat my dad had made with superglue and a feather. When making the hat, Dad somehow managed to glue himself to the wall by a single finger, so Mum had to squeeze warm water from a sponge on to it in

order to release him. I'd been in a grump all day, because the hat
kept unsticking and my outfit was ruined. There was a little hole
in the middle of my tights, which one of the girls in the chippy
pointed out by wiggling her finger into it, telling me to be careful
a bird didn't nip my tail. It had been a fancy-dress day at school,
and I took these things seriously. I've always loved dressing up, as
did my father. He'd often come to the door wrapped in colourful
scarves like a fortune teller. My sisters and I would be thrilled as
a hand emerged from the swathes of fabric, and he handed us a
chocolate orange. We'd dance around the living room together,
eating segments of it. I think those experiences, and the fact that
Dad took me to drama classes from the age of three, fostered my
love for performance. So, when *Strictly Come Dancing* came along
years later, you can only imagine how excited I was to wear those
sequins.

But despite my willingness to perform, I can't remember a
time when I wasn't conscious of how I looked. One morning,
when I was about eight, Mum was driving me to school when I
clocked myself in the rear-view mirror and threw a hysterical fit.
At the time, my fine blond locks resembled a dandelion clock if
they weren't dampened and perfectly combed into a side parting,
and I'd forgotten to wet my hair. I made such a fuss that Mum had
to stop at the side of the road and use the water from a puddle. I
wonder now if these were early signs of my eating disorder and
body dysmorphia. Would it have been possible to tell that in just
a few years, I'd start following fad diets and monitoring calories,
and shortly after that start making myself sick in an attempt to

control my image? Or did everything begin even earlier than that? Were my demons inbuilt from birth?

I was always experimenting with my looks throughout both primary and high school. In fact, I'd go as far as to say I was obsessed with image. I don't think it was in a vain way, but it was certainly in an effort to garner attention and validation. If I wasn't rinsing a 'hint-of-a-tint' semi-permanent colour through my hair, I was shaving a checkerboard pattern into it and dyeing it black and white. I see the error of my ways now – of course I do. And my impulse is to look back at that lad with anger: what was missing in my life to warrant such attention-seeking behaviour? But what would that achieve? It would only add to the shame.

All this did get me attention, but it was mostly negative. One particular teacher would snarl at me and call me a 'stupid lad' when I sported a new colour or cut. Boys in the playground would continue to hurl their homophobic slurs.

But it wasn't just the boys. I remember one night at a friend's sleepover, when my three girlfriends suddenly turned on me: 'You're gay. We know you're gay because of the way you walk and the way you hold your schoolbag.' I couldn't believe how they attacked me, like a pack of dogs. I had to flee the house – and it was straight to the chip shop that I ran for help. We didn't own it by this time, but I knew the people who had taken over, and they kindly drove me home. Mum couldn't come for me, as she'd been out for dinner with friends and had drunk a glass of wine.

Why I dyed my hair, I don't know. Perhaps something was

missing. Perhaps I knew I'd never be like the other lads and so needed to own that distinction. But I remember the feeling of disgust when I found myself aroused by the men's underwear section of the Next catalogue and the magazines my sisters left on the bathroom floor, which featured ripped blokes in tiny underpants. I'd lock myself in there and spend hours turning the pages, lusting after the bodies and bulges. Their physiques were all rolling with muscle, and while I found it alluring, I'd stare in the mirror at my 'puppy fat', as my drama teacher called it, and uneven shoulders, slowly developing a hatred for my size and shape. My face was round and smooth, and my teeth – my dominoes as my sister joked – were too big for my face. My fat pear-shaped belly hung over my underpants. The only thing I liked about my face was the freckle under my eye, invisible to anyone at distance, which was everyone.

Shame bubbles up from deep within. It's like a fire that is stoked by bigotry and bullying, but when you're burning in those flames, you don't see past the internal. You truly believe you deserve to feel this way. I hated myself. I could see the way other people saw me, and I allowed myself to have the same low opinion. If I could go back and help that little lad, I'd hug him so tightly. I'd shout loudly so everyone else could hear: what you are is unique and beautiful. What you are is normal and acceptable. What you are is who you are supposed to be, and you deserve to be loved just like every other person on this planet. But the boy I was at that age only heard what the bigots and bullies had to say. It was commonplace for things that were negative or boring or dull or unwanted to be labelled as 'gay'. If a lad didn't want to do something in class it would be, 'Oh, but Miss, that's gay, that is.'

Gay was negative. Gay was what people wanted to avoid.

* * *

There was plenty of fun in my childhood, though. The chip shop – a 1950s prefab shed that was bitterly cold in the winter, until, of course, the fryers were in full operation, at which point it would become unbearably hot and condensation would drip down the windows and walls – was such a wonderful place for a kid. The floor was so slippery. I remember how Dad would run from the potato room with a yellow bucket of freshly cut chips, his golden hair flapping on the back of his head as he tried to steady his march like an angry chicken. We used to wrap the fish and chips in paper, and we'd put some sheets of this paper on the tiles to serve as stepping stones across the slick surface. He'd always skid all over the place all the same, and then, as though at a bowling alley, he'd slide the bucket of chips along the floor and into the corner, never once spilling any. Whenever I tried to achieve the same feat, I'd bang my shoulder on the microwave or knock my head on the shelf just beneath the window where the brews were made.

My friends were always so intrigued by the fact we had a chip shop. One lad couldn't get his head around the idea that we didn't live there: 'So, you *own* the chip shop, but you live somewhere else?' he'd ask. I don't know why it was so difficult for him; you'd only need to take one look at the rickety shack, with its single-glazed windows and what was probably an asbestos roof, to know that living there wouldn't be possible. We lived in a little detached house on an estate nearby, with other working-class families. When I was really little – three or four – I'd stand on the end of our drive shouting 'get off my land' to the boys from a few doors down. One time I even cut out a photograph of a steak knife and held it up swearing as they cycled past. Their mother, Julie, always threatened to wash my mouth out with Fairy Liquid if I didn't stop with the language. I'd get her back by pulling the streamer branches off her weeping willow tree when she wasn't around. I liked her. I found a sense of safety in bolshie women.

If I wasn't terrorising the estate, like a three-feet-tall, white-blonde dictator, I'd mostly be playing at the chippy. At the very back edge of the plot of land was a huge old beech tree, which overhung onto the school playing field. I named the tree Ernie, and would spend hours just sat up in it alone, watching the other kids play in summer school. Inside the shop, when I was about six or seven, the pea barrel was my favourite place. It was a big black bucket full of dried peas. I'd sink my hands and arms into it as deeply as I could, trying to bury myself completely. I'd scoop up the little muted-green orbs with a jug and let them tumble back into bucket – the clattering sound would soothe me and give me goosebumps on my arms. In summer, I'd take cups of peas outside and let them rattle around on the concrete. They'd dart about the floor and I'd make patterns. I got into trouble quite a few times for clogging the drains with peas. One spring, some pea shoots started to emerge from beneath the drainpipe. I remember

Mum shouting at me as she dredged the drains with her hands, her cheeks pink with stress. I found it so marvellous how Mum would soak the peas (definitely not the ones from the drain!) overnight in water and bicarbonate of soda, then boil them the next day to make the mushy peas. We'd often sample them on a slice of bread, seasoned with plenty of salt and vinegar, to make sure the taste was just right to serve to the customers. Absolutely delicious.

* * *

She was a hard-working woman, my mum, and determined to give us a better life than the one she'd had. The eldest of three siblings, and the only girl, her early childhood had been one of hardship. It was the kind of household where if the cat had a litter of kittens, they would be drowned in a hessian sack, as there just weren't the resources to feed any extra mouths. Times were hard, and such times force people to be hard, too.

Although just a longstanding family joke, it wasn't difficult to believe (in my case for years) the story about when the vicar came to visit. My mum and her brother, my uncle Karl were upstairs in bed. They had only an overcoat as a bed cover and my mum shouted down, 'Mum, Karl's got his leg stuck in the arm of the overcoat!'

My embarrassed grandma shouted back, 'It's a duvet, dear!', to which Mum replied, 'OK, Karl's got his leg stuck in the arm of the duvet.' I shouldn't have found it so easy to believe; Mum's side has never been religious.

Humour aside, looking back now that I'm no longer a petulant, self-centred child, she must have been knackered. What I saw then as a mother who was always too busy or too distracted for us, was, in fact, a woman hellbent on giving her children the best opportunities she could. She never stopped, and only in recent years, since she suffered a life-changing accident, has she allowed herself to slow down and enjoy life a little more.

But back then, I was adamant that Mum didn't love me, and no one could have told me otherwise. Of course I see now just how deeply she did love me and my sisters. My thoughts and feelings simply weren't fact, but children don't need fact to feel. Fantasy is a more powerful conjurer of emotion.

Mum's father, Merrick, was a remarkable man, always looking for a way to better himself. He loved kids – I remember him squirting squirty cream from a can all the way up my arms, laughing as I struggled to lick it off, and it was he who taught me about the winning combination of cottage cheese and jam on toast – but he certainly wasn't above getting his children to help him. From the age of seven, Mum had accompanied him on his milk round. Whatever the weather, they went up every driveway to deliver milk to their customers. With any spare money he earned, he started doing up cars, and used the profit he made from selling them to buy and renovate terrace houses. Eventually, he saved enough to buy a farm. In the first year of owning it, he took turf off the fields to sell to help clear his mortgage, and as the turf business grew to be successful, he opened a kennel and a fishing lake.

It was Merrick who came to my parents' aid when the

chipper – the machine that turned the spuds into chips – gave up one hectic Friday teatime (dinnertime if you're posh; suppertime if you're verging on aristocratic). After a quick phone call, my grandad arrived with a contraption that clipped on to the stainless-steel workbench. It had a great, stiff lever that pressed down on to one potato at a time, forcing it through a mesh plate and slicing it into chips. I remember his massive, hairy hands pushing on the lever. Those hands were the painting of the years of his hard labour. It was physical, back-breaking work when a crowd of hungry villagers were waiting impatiently in the next room, so we – my sisters, Grandad and me – all took it in turns to make the chips while Mum and Dad continued to fry and serve customers.

I didn't appreciate until later the work ethic that this instilled in me. Seeing my grandad and mum refuse to let their customers down or lose vital income made me constantly conscious of the importance of always *doing* something. Sometimes that can be a bad thing – even when I'm ill, I find it hard to just lie there and watch television. There's a fine line between work ethic and work shame. One is a positive driving force that enables a person to clamber out of bed in the morning and say, 'Hey world, I'm going to do something with my life for *me*!' The other – shame – is an externally derived weight that forces a person compare themselves to others and ask, 'Am I doing enough? Should I be working harder than I am?' I try my hardest when having a well-earned day off to quieten the work shame that bubbles up and use my work ethic to balance it; I've worked hard to this point, and to carry on working hard, I must rest, recuperate and relax.

It perplexes me now how, even when going through her divorce from my father, Mum continued to work. She never stopped. In the holidays, or when the shop was shut on a Monday, she'd drive us in her little white Corsa to the chippy and we'd clean it, just me and her, from top to bottom. I'd get mad at her for making me work all the time, and infuriated when she wouldn't listen to me. She was once trimming the fish in the back of the chippy and I was trying to tell her something. When she didn't respond, I kicked off. I must have pushed her too far, because, still clutching the fish knife, she said something along the lines of, 'Say that again, and I'll kill you.' It wasn't an actual threat, just an attempt to regain control by a woman who was at the end of her tether. I burst through the door and into the customer area, screaming, 'She's got a knife. She's going to kill me!'

The builders waiting for their sausage, chips, peas and gravy didn't bat an eyelid: northern stoicism at its best. One even murmured, 'Aye, I'd kill you if you wo' mine, yer little bastard!'

We did have some fun times, me and Mum. Sometimes we'd draw little cartoons on the wrapping paper, or share sweets and ice creams on the grass in the hot sun. When going through a difficult stage in my behaviour, she'd use the chip paper to explain the importance of putting others first. She'd write the word 'joy' vertically down the page, then use that to demonstrate if you put *J*esus and *O*thers before *Y*ourself, you'd be happy. Though she too admitted it was a little bit of a strain for her to use that particular example due to her lack of belief in a god. But it worked well to illustrate the message, that agnostic acrostic.

It was Mum who taught me how to make a volcano. She'd invert a chip cone on a tray, take off the tip, fill it with bicarbonate of soda – of which we had an abundant supply, thanks to our constant production of mushy peas – then pour in the vinegar. The reaction between acid and alkaline would cause a great, pressurised fizz that would spurt out of the cone and down the sides. I must have got through hundreds of chip cones during our time there – I practically recreated the formation of the world in polystyrene and acid-alkali fizz.

★ ★ ★

It was in the chip shop that I first had the feeling my world was about to crumble, and that I was going to lose Mum for ever, as a new man came on to the scene: my future stepdad. I knew about him, because I'd sit on Mum's bed as she got ready to go out after she and Dad divorced. I remember the smell of her perfume – Yvresse by Yves Saint Laurent – and the goosebumps I'd get on my arms from the white noise of her hairdryer. I can still feel the sting of her Lipcote lipstick sealer on my lips after she kissed me goodbye.

After we had finished a shift one evening, I was plonked on the counter to keep my feet off the freshly mopped floor, when the door opened and a stern-looking man walked in. He was dressed like a typical 1990s farmer: corduroy trousers, checked shirt, oversized tweed jacket and flat cap, with gigantic thick spectacles. I can't remember how Mum introduced him – she wouldn't have said boyfriend, because that would have been weird, but she made it clear she was dating him.

Once I realised he was a permanent fixture, I became an acid-tongued viper. 'You're not my real dad!' I hissed at him, as he stood there awkwardly, saying nothing. 'You're not going to steal my mummy!' I summoned all the hurtful things a six-year-old could possibly say and hurled them at this stranger. I can still taste the rage I felt. I was a brat. I was nasty. I would have clawed away at the mud, desperate to find a single stone with which to take him down.

I was a scared little boy.

* * *

I worked in the chippy for years, up until we sold the business. As you'd imagine, the staff were rather more interested in the chips themselves than the volcanic potential of chip cones. I remember the girls who worked there dousing their plump portions in obscene amounts of salt and vinegar; curiously, though, they were all always on diets. There was a calorie-counting book behind the till, which my mum, my sister Jane and the other girls would use every day. One of the girls once had a can of Weight Watchers soup, into which she dunked a sausage barm cake. Jane laughed and told her that wasn't what you were supposed to do.

Dad was quite openly vocal about his dislike for fat people. He would say how disgusting it was for a person to allow themselves to get so big. I don't think I realised the impact this had on my sense of what a normal body shape and size were. I certainly digested that opinion and used it – not in an outward way towards other people, but inwardly, towards myself. It was another missile in my armoury of self-loathing.

All this meant I grew up thinking diets were normal, and so during high school, if I wasn't counting calories, I'd be restricting my carbohydrate intake. I think seeing the girls so obsessed with what they ate and how it affected their bodies was undoubtedly one of the contributors to my own struggles with food. Despite growing up in a chippy, I didn't really like fish and chips – I do now, but I have to *really* crave them. I always found the batter too rich and the chips too bland. Mindful, too, of calories, I'd refuse to eat the chips and battered fish, and opt instead for steamed fish with mushy peas; then I'd happily walk to the filling station and spend a pound or two on pick 'n' mix sweets.

Whenever I did allow myself something other than steamed fish, my favourite indulgent treat was a mushy pea barm cake, which my sister Jane introduced me to: a well-buttered (though really it was margarine) barm cake filled with mushy peas that had been allowed to drain in the scoop slightly to remove some of the excess moisture. If the lads in the village hadn't cycled to the window of the chippy to take the scraps of batter as a free snack, we'd sprinkle those on top too, then absolutely souse it all in proper chip-shop vinegar – which isn't actually vinegar at all, but rather a 'non-brewed condiment' of acetic acid mixed with water and colourings.

There was something about the fluffy bread and greasy marg that married so well with the smooth, almost creamy, mushy peas and the crunch of the batter. It was proper northern sloppy food, with the bottom half of the bread getting so soaked you'd need to finish eating it with one of those blue plastic takeaway forks.

I also loved a cheese and onion pie, but I would have done anything for a steak and kidney pudding. I'd scoop out the meaty interior and eat it spoonful by spoonful, saving the soggy suet pastry until last, tearing pieces off and eating it with my fingers. Sometimes I'd even put the soaked pastry, free of the filling, on a slice of buttered bread. Now, *that* was a treat!

I'd enjoy watching as the girls plucked the puddings from the towering steamer with their fingertips and tossed them from hand to hand as they carried them to the serving area, before inverting them in the polystyrene chip trays and slapping them on the base to remove the foil. The trick was to slap them quickly but lightly, so that the pastry would release from the mould without rupturing. Being the heavy-handed brute that I am, I'd always leave a tray of total evisceration, and would need to ask Mum or Jane to do another one for me. I had, by this point, been promoted from potato-peeler to customer-server, which I hated, because I felt the judging eyes of the tradesmen. While in the safety of our own home we were just another working-class family, here we were on show – a spectacle; minor celebrities of this insular little village where nothing much ever happened. We weren't just serving customers, we were on stage, performing to entertain while sometimes fifteen people or more awaited their food, all facing towards us, watching our every move. I had to work the crowd, but entirely on the crowd's terms. I had to make myself palatable and acceptable, to fit in. The girls in the shop would flirt and fawn over the lads as they cleaned down after we'd closed. 'He's so fit!', they'd giggle. I wanted to join in, tell them how beautiful I thought his eyes were, how I liked his big hands and would trace the wrinkles beside his eyes when he smiled at me as I handed him the change. But instead, I bit my lip to act with closeted choreographed precision: a dance on eggshells.

Brined Chips

_____

SERVES 2

If I'd suggested brining the chips before frying them back in the chippy days, my parents and the other workers would have undoubtedly laughed in my face. New-fangled approaches just weren't welcome, and I think there's a certain comfort in that. Sticking to what you know – a process that has never let you down – gives you certainty, and with certainty can come happiness. While I do appreciate repetition, I also fear stagnation and like to break away from it, so I dabbled in brining my chips – a practice quite popular in some trendy eateries across the world. It makes the chips more flavourful, of course, but also a little fluffier in texture, because the bacteria in the fermentation process starts to break down the flesh of the potato. Bear in mind that you'll need to brine the potatoes for at least four days. It's worth it.

500g (1lb 2oz) Maris Piper potatoes, peeled
15g (½oz) sea salt flakes

- Cut the potatoes into 1cm (½in) chips. If you have to get out a ruler to help you do this precisely, then do it. If you're happy to be a little more haphazard and random, then good for you.

Put the chips into a bowl and toss with the salt. Leave for 20 minutes for the salt to draw out moisture from the potatoes and dissolve, then pour in enough water to cover them. Cover with a clean tea towel and leave at room temperature, out of direct sunlight, for 4–5 days, until the bowl smells slightly sour and there's perhaps a little fizz dotting the water.

- Drain the brine from the chips, but don't rinse them with fresh water – just let them sit in a colander in the sink to drain well. Dab them with a clean tea towel, too, to remove excess surface moisture.

To deep-fry the chips

vegetable oil, for frying
salt and vinegar, to serve

- Fill a deep-fat fryer with vegetable oil and preheat it to 130°C (266°F). When the oil is hot, put the chips into the fryer and cook for about 6 minutes, until soft but uncoloured.

- Lift up the draining basket and allow the chips to sit above the fryer while you increase the heat of the oil to 180°C (356°F). Once it reaches this temperature, drop the basket back in, giving it a little shake every now and again so the chips don't stick, and fry for about 4 minutes or until they are very lightly golden and crispy. Drain the chips, then tip them into a bowl to toss with salt and vinegar before serving.

To oven-roast the chips

2 tablespoons olive oil
salt and vinegar, to serve

• If you fancy making the chips a little lighter, try roasting them. Preheat the oven to 200°C/180°C fan/400°F/gas mark 6. Put the drained chips into a bowl, then add the olive oil and toss together. Scatter them over a baking sheet, spacing them well apart – any that overlap won't cook, so give them space. Roast for 20 minutes, then increase the oven temperature to 240°C/220°C fan/475°F/gas mark 9 and bake for a further 10–12 minutes or until the chips are a very pale golden colour, but extremely crispy.

• Toss with a little salt and vinegar in a generously sized bowl, then serve.

Simple Mushy Peas

———

MAKES ENOUGH FOR A SMALL CROWD

I can't think about the chippy without my mind almost immediately flicking to the black vat of dried marrowfat peas, with which I'd play for hours. It stood right beneath the telephone, so if I ever chatted to a friend or my grandma on the phone, my fingers would certainly be stroking the surface of the peas.

This recipe is simple – completely no frills. I have suggested the addition of miso paste if you want to amp up the flavour, but that's only if the earthy, sweet simplicity of mushy peas isn't enough for you. If the idea of throwing in anything else is sacrilegious, please ignore the suggestion and don't take offence (I know how protective northerners can get when it comes to gravy and mushy peas!). If you're going to embark on this mushy pea pilgrimage, please bear in mind you'll need to soak them overnight before cooking.

1 tablespoon bicarbonate of soda (baking soda)
250g (9oz) dried marrowfat peas
juice of ½ lemon
sea salt flakes

- Put the bicarbonate of soda into a large mixing bowl and add 1 litre (1¾ pints) boiling water. Give it a stir to dissolve the bicarb (although it should almost instantly dissolve anyway), then add the peas. They should be fairly well covered by the water – by a good thumb's depth – so if they're not, add more water (cold or hot, it doesn't matter). Leave for at least 12 hours – 18 is better.

- Once the peas have soaked, drain them and rinse them well. Mum always made sure we checked them well for micro stones. I think I only ever found one, so the chances are slim, but ritual is more sacred than reason. Put the rinsed peas into a large pan and cover with about 1.2 litres (2 pints) water – they should be submerged by maybe just over half a thumb this time. Add the lemon juice. This will cause the water to fizz, because of the residual bicarbonate of soda in the pea flesh, but that's a good thing – it'll make them softer.

- Place over a high heat and bring to the boil, then reduce to a simmer. Cook for 25–40 minutes, or until the peas are very mushy and the consistency you like – I like them *very* thick, but please do remember that, as with most starchy and gloopy foods, they'll thicken as they sit there, and even more so as they cool. Season with salt to taste.

Miso Mushy Peas

If these had been offered on the chip-shop menu, the builders, truckers and Friday teatime families would probably have laughed in sheer confusion. But, as I've started to become more obsessed with fermented foods, I have to say with all honesty that, for me, they're bloody delicious. Simply add spoonfuls of white miso paste to taste. Don't start off too heavy-handed, because it can pack a punch (and nor is it the cheapest thing to buy). You can top up the umami flavour with some Worcestershire sauce, too.

Barm Cakes for Mushy Pea Barms

———

MAKES 6

I don't even want to get into the regional debate about what these are called. Whether you call them barm cakes, muffins, baps or rolls, it doesn't matter one iota to me – just shut up and eat them. And I mean that instruction with nothing but the stern love of a Lancashire chippy owner.

80g (2¾oz) milk
80g (2¾oz) tepid water
10g (¼oz) caster (superfine) sugar
5g (⅛oz) fast-action dried yeast
30g (1oz) unsalted butter, at room temperature
250g (9oz) strong white bread flour, plus extra for dusting
5g (⅛oz) fine salt
flavourless oil (such as sunflower), for greasing

• If you're using a freestanding electric mixer with a dough hook attachment, then pop the milk, water, sugar, yeast and butter into the mixing bowl and stir together briefly. Scatter the flour and salt on top, then, holding the dough hook in your hand, start to bring everything together. This stops the machine acting too vigorously in the first stage of mixing together the wet and dry ingredients, and therefore avoids an almighty explosion of flour. Put the hook and bowl on to the mixer and knead on a medium speed for about 8 minutes, or until the dough is elastic and smooth. To test the dough is ready, take a walnut-sized chunk, dip it liberally in some flour, then very carefully tease it and stretch it with well-floured fingers. If you can get it very thin, like a membrane or windowpane, without more than one or two minor tears in it, then it is ready. If not, continue to knead.

- If you're doing this by hand, throw the ingredients into a mixing bowl and stir together into a thick paste using a wooden spoon, then tip on to the worktop and knead until smooth and elastic – this will normally take 10–15 minutes, so roll up your sleeves and crack on. If you're not used to kneading bread by hand, I urge you to put this book down, wash your hands, make a cup of tea using the method described at the very beginning of this book and watch a few YouTube videos on the subject. I know that seems like I'm shirking responsibility here, but I'm not. I want you to learn, and cooking is an utterly visual thing. And while you're at it, watch a video on the visual of the windowpane test, as mentioned above.

- Once the dough has been sufficiently kneaded, grease a mixing bowl with oil and coat the dough in it. Cover with a clean tea towel and leave to rise until doubled in size – how long this will take depends entirely on how warm your kitchen is. I may as well live in the Arctic circle, it's that bloody cold in my house, so I turn on the oven light, put a tray of boiling water at the bottom of the oven, then put my dough in there, still covered and in the bowl. This creates a warm, damp environment where the yeast can do its thing and helps the dough rise that bit more quickly – with this method, it should rise in 45–60 minutes.

- Once the dough has risen, knock it back (just punch it to remove the air), then divide it evenly into six portions. I insist you weigh the bulk of the dough and then divide that weight by six – you've come this far, so why would you want to take shortcuts now? By my calculations, the dough portions should each weigh about 75g (2⅔oz).

- On a very lightly floured worktop, shape the portions into neat balls: press each one down into a flat disc, then bring the edges of the disc up and over into the centre of the dough, pressing them down firmly to stick them in place – it should look a bit like a scraggy wonton dumpling. Continue doing this to build up resistance in the dough, then flip it over so the smooth, neat side is on top, and carefully but forcibly rotate it against the worktop with one hand to make the little sphere of dough even tighter.

- Pop the dough balls on to a baking sheet that has been lined with baking paper (parchment paper), spacing them out so they have room to puff up. Dust with a little flour (I don't bother to cover them with clingfilm/plastic wrap or anything) then leave to double in size again, either at room temperature or using the same technique as above. I find it helps to take a photograph on my phone to use as a comparator when the dough balls have risen – that way, I'm able to see precisely how much bigger they are.

- Once they've doubled in size, remove the tray from the oven (if you proved them in there), then preheat the oven to 220°C/200°C fan/425°F/gas mark 7. Bake the barm cakes for 10 minutes, or until they are golden brown and sound hollow when firmly tapped on the bottom. Transfer to a wire rack and allow to cool underneath a clean tea towel to make the crusts lovely and soft.

- To serve as a mushy pea barm, slice the barm cakes open, spread liberally with a salty butter, then pile on the mushy peas and sprinkle with salt and vinegar (ideally the 'non-brewed condiment' kind that chip shops serve, though a malt will just about do it).

Jacket Potato Three Ways

Towards the end of our time at the chippy, Mum invested in a Queen Victoria jacket potato oven – a huge black enamel box with a glass-paned warming unit at the top. It towered austerely on the counter, full of jacket potatoes. I found it to be quite an oppressive thing: old-fashioned and rigid, rather like how I then saw my stepdad, who came into our lives at around the same time.

Like fish and chips, I never understood the appeal of the jacket spud – I always found them a little too cocksure for such a wonky, bland lump. I didn't understand why people fawned over them. While I'd still take a roast potato any day, soused in vinegar and glistening under a pool of melted garlic butter, I now appreciate the opportunity a jacket potato brings – like a good sourdough pizza base, it is a vessel for flavour.

The Jacket Potato

baking potatoes – as many as you want to bake
oil (I use sunflower or rapeseed)
fine salt

• Rub the skins of your potatoes in oil and salt, then pop them straight on to the top rack of the cold oven – no need to waste energy preheating. Turn the oven on to 240°C/220°C fan/475°F/gas mark 9. As soon as the oven reaches this temperature, turn it down to 190°C/170°C fan/375°F/gas mark 5 and bake for 45–50 minutes, or until the skins are golden and the insides are mushy. If you have an instant-read digital thermometer, the perfect internal temperature for a jacket potato is 97–99°C (207–210°F).

- The potatoes, once cooled, can be stored in an airtight container in the fridge for up to 5 days. Just reheat in a hot oven for 15–20 minutes.

Chippy Tea Jacket Potato
SERVES 2

2 jacket potatoes, cooked using the recipe above
6 battered fish fingers
4 tablespoons tartare sauce
300g (10½oz) mushy peas (homemade, see page 30,
or use a can of Batchelors)
salt and vinegar

- Fifteen minutes before the potatoes are due to finish baking, pop the fish fingers on to a baking tray and into the oven, and bake until crispy.

- When the potatoes are ready, cut them in half and scoop out the flesh into a bowl, leaving the skins intact. Roughly chop four of the fish fingers and mash them with the potato flesh, 2 tablespoons of the tartare sauce and a generous pinch of salt. Don't mash them smooth – leave plenty of texture. Scoop this mashed mixture back in to the potato skins.

• Heat the peas (in the microwave, a pan or to packet instructions, if using a tin) and pour them over the potatoes, then flake the remaining fish fingers on top. Dollop on the remaining tartare sauce and finish with a generous drenching of salt and vinegar.

Curried Beans Jacket Potato
SERVES 2

2 jacket potatoes, cooked using the recipe above
415g (14½oz) can baked beans
1½ tablespoons jalfrezi curry paste
2 tablespoons cottage cheese
2 tablespoons raita
4 teaspoons mango chutney
2 poppadoms, crushed
1 green chilli, finely chopped
2 spring onions, finely sliced

• While the potatoes are in their last 10 minutes of baking, put the beans and curry paste into a saucepan and set over a medium heat. Stir as the beans come to the boil.

- When the potatoes are ready, cut a deep cross into each baked one and squeeze the four sections together. Dollop the cottage cheese into the potatoes and top with the beans, then finish with the raita, mango chutney, crushed poppadom and a scattering of chilli and spring onions.

Bacon, Cheddar and Apple Sauce
SERVES 2

2 jacket potatoes, cooked using the recipe above
8 rashers smoked streaky bacon, roughly chopped
2 spring onions, finely chopped
8 teaspoons apple sauce
60g (2¼oz) mature Cheddar, grated
salt and pepper

- When the potatoes are in their last 15 minutes of baking, lay the bacon rashers on a baking tray and transfer to the oven. Bake for 10–15 minutes until crispy – or however you like your bacon.

- When the potatoes are ready, let them cool slightly, then cut them in half and carefully scoop the flesh into a bowl, leaving the skins intact. Add three-quarters of the chopped bacon to the bowl of potato flesh, along with the spring onions, 2 teaspoons of the apple sauce and a generous pinch of salt and pepper. Mix everything together well, then scoop the filling back into the potato skins – I find it helpful to pop the skins into a muffin tin to stop them from wobbling all over the place.

- Top with the grated cheese and pop under the grill for a few minutes. Finish by dolloping on the remaining apple sauce and scattering over the remaining chopped bacon.

2.
Not at the Table

———

I don't know if love for animals is instinct, learned behaviour or a blend of both, but after my parents had divorced and we began spending more time at my future stepdad's farm, it was the animals that gave me comfort in a place I sometimes found frightening.

Before that, the first creatures in my life were Rusty and Squeak, my sisters' guinea pigs. I don't think I played with them much, but I certainly remember when they died within days of each other – loneliness and heartbreak often kill the second of a pair of guinea pigs. I can't have been more than two years old, but I remember the funeral we held in the back garden. Dad dug a hole (not far from the apple tree in which he eventually built me my treehouse – Apple Tree Cottage), put the guinea pigs into a shoebox and buried them beneath the plum tree. I think my sisters made a headstone out of a cassette tape box.

That's one thing for which I'll be forever grateful to my

parents: they never shielded us from the ultimate certainty of death or tried to sugar-coat the reality. When my snowy-white cat, Alastair, always covered in lesions from having feline immunodeficiency virus, met his maker, he didn't 'move to a lovely farm'; he was simply squashed flat in the Windmill pub car park. I'll never forget crying in the bath, clutching his tatty old collar. When the stick insects were found crispy and well dead in a jam jar at the back of my sister Victoria's knicker drawer, they weren't flushed down the toilet in secret; we peered at them through the glass, just to make sure they'd definitely expired. We were allowed, even encouraged, to mourn that sadness and loss, to feel the painful sting at the negative end of the spectrum of our sentiment. And there was something quite reassuring about knowing that sacred truth. Other children's animals 'moved in with another family'; ours died.

Apart from Claud, the garlic-bread-eating cat.

After a few years on the farm, we were allowed to have cats. I came home from primary school one day to find a white bucket with a hole in the lid plonked at the foot of the stairs. I ripped off the lid and, with the same force, a tiny grey-and-white cat jumped out and scratched fiercely at me. For days, he'd cower underneath the sideboard, only for me to drag him out by the scruff of his neck in an effort to acclimatise him to both us and the house. It took a bold fearlessness matched with a gentle and encouraging love to bring him round. I'd lock him in the bathroom at night and make little houses for him out of cardboard boxes, and within weeks, he was a fat domestic cat. My attempts at taming him were tallied by the scratches on my arms – how I didn't end up with tetanus, I'll never know – but what I did end up with was a loving companion.

Claud was with us for many years, but when we came back from holiday one year, he was gone. We assumed he was dead, but as we didn't have a body, we didn't hold a feline funeral. A few months later, we learned he'd moved into a house belonging to a man who played rugby for Wigan Warriors – his family had been feeding him chicken and milk while we were away. I don't blame Claud; I could easily be lured away from my family by the juicy tenderness of a roast chicken. Some time later, I was being driven to a high school leaving party when we found him in the middle of the road, bloodied and struggling to breathe – clearly a hit and run. I leapt from the car in my posh party clothes and fell to my knees beside him. I held him on my lap and nursed him until he took his final breath.

We delivered Claud's body back to the house of his adopted family. The mother, distraught and worried about what to tell her children – all much younger than me – was comforted by my wise and matter-of-fact mum, who told her: 'Tell them the truth and have a funeral for him – it'll give them the chance to say goodbye.'

Although he left me for a while, I like to tell myself that something greater brought Claud and me back together for his final moments. That distance, I guess, showed me that love, in its physical form, sometimes disappears or moves on to someone else, but like the ebb and flow of a tide, it never truly ends. This was true of my dad, too, who by this time was someone I just didn't see as much. It's tormenting to have someone you love so deeply plucked away from you. It makes you question your love for them at times. Dad was the only man I would kiss goodnight, so not to have him here with me, his strong hands tucking me in, as I brushed my hands in his stubble for the final time each day, was fucking painful. Who would give me daily guidance in the subtle art of becoming a man? The cat?

While I felt there was no one to tame me, I certainly tamed Claud, and, in return, he – and his black-and-white cousin, Pixie, who curiously died at another important transition of my life: around the time I moved out to my university flat in Manchester – gave me many years of companionship in a house that otherwise filled me with fear. My dear friend Lucy, a senior lecturer in psychology at the University of West England and author of *No Family Is Perfect: A Guide to Embracing the Messy Reality*, told me: 'Creatures mean everything to us when humans are complex: our pets always have time and love for us – not all humans can do that when they're stressed or anxious or have pressures and challenges to face.'

★ ★ ★

The farm was a terrifying house for a young child; even now, the thought of it makes me feel an urgent and desperate discomfort – the kind that makes you want to shed your skin and flee the country. It was a converted barn on a dairy farm, with high, vaulted ceilings in the bedrooms and exposed beams, freckled with woodworm holes. My sister and stepbrother told me – for their own amusement, I suppose – that an old farmer had hanged himself from the beams in my bedroom, and from that moment, the entire place filled me with fear. Haunted, I'd stay up at night for as long as I could – sometimes all night. I felt a loneliness in those dark hours that still chills me. I was *so* afraid. I'd often try to sneak into one of my sisters' bedrooms at night and sleep on the floor. Sometimes they wouldn't wake up, and I'd make it until morning, safe and comforted by their presence. But too often, the creak of the door or floorboards would jolt them, and they'd shout, 'Get out, John!'

If I was banished from their bedrooms, I'd sleep on the floor outside their doors, and they'd have to step over me – a human draft excluder – on their way down to breakfast. Alternatively, I'd stay up all night in my room, with the lights on. Sometimes I was too petrified to leave the room, so I'd piss out of the window or into a towel on the floor. An uncle had bought me a VHS of the American sitcom *Friends*, which I'd watch from beginning to end, then rewind and repeat until I fell asleep. To this day, I watch *Friends* most evenings to help me drift off. I know it word for word, and it will always be a great source of comfort to me.

If I wasn't watching *Friends* or reading the *Chronicle of the 20th Century* over and over, I'd pile up the spare pillows on the edge of my bed to create a little den or nest. That way, if I did fall asleep and woke up to a room full of spectres, I wouldn't be able to see them for the protective duvet canopy above my head.

Looking back, it wasn't just the old stone barn that prevented me sleeping – as scary as it was. Even if I was at Dad's house, or his new partner's, I'd need him to sleep in the bunkbeds with me. Perhaps it was a way of coping with the division in my family; maybe ghosts don't haunt children, and divorces do. But if my sisters were going out for the night, I'd ask to sleep at Dad's. He made me feel safe, as we'd eat jelly sweets watching *Gimme Gimme Gimme*, laughing in shock at the profanity of the show.

At the farm I'd beg to leave the hall light on, but my stepdad would insist I turned it off, because it would shine through the crack in his bedroom door and keep him awake. Mum would quietly tell me to turn it on in the middle of the night when everyone was asleep – she knew once he was out for the count, nothing would wake him.

★ ★ ★

She was good like that, my mum. She wasn't really one to confront a situation head-on – whenever she could, she'd avoid the conflict – but she'd find ways of making me feel that bit safer. When I was bullied at high school for being 'the fat fucking gay boy', she never approached the teachers about it, but she'd happily write a letter to excuse me from PE, knowing that being in such concentrated proximity to a gang of lads could be devastating to me. When I got blindingly pissed at a college fancy-dress party, she didn't bollock me as I'd anticipated, but instead cut me out of my Edward Scissorhands costume. I had made it out of skin-tight black clothes, belts and a whole roll of black duct tape. I was so drunk that night I weed on my friend's leg, and Mum had to pick me up – all six foot two of me – carry me to my room, cut me out of my clothes, then sleep on the floor beside me so I didn't choke on my own vomit.

She'd tell me to fight back, which I often did. I was always getting into scraps with the lads who called me names. I don't condone violence, but I certainly condone defence. And I think that made me aware of justice from an early age. I wouldn't say I'm grateful to the lads who called me names at school, but it was certainly refreshing to repeat their taunts of 'Chase me through the forest' as a little inspiration during a playful dance on one of the biggest television shows in the country, *Strictly Come Dancing*. That was far more powerful than a punch to the ribcage. But punches to the ribs I pulled aplenty. Some of the teachers told me they were proud of me for sticking up for myself – on the quiet, of course.

Many of the teachers were life-savers – and I don't use that term without due consideration of its deep meaning. They were all women. They could see the anguish in me as I came to terms with my sexuality, and they knew that I wasn't fully able to express it without fear of persecution. They were protective of me: my form tutor, my German teacher, my English teacher. They were a loving contrast to some others, who would literally yell in my face, their nose almost touching mine, because I'd dyed my hair blue or red. There was a learning support tutor – whose name I cannot recall – who once dragged me from beneath a lad after we'd got into a fight. I wish I could thank her. She might have been a tiny thing but she certainly ferreted her way into this ball of tangled testosterone as it thrashed around the playground.

She held on to me so tightly and walked me to the headmaster, whispering, 'I've got you, lad, I've got you!' as I gritted my teeth to hold back the tears.

★ ★ ★

It was Dad who helped ease my fear of sleeping alone. When he slept in my room, he always told me that at some point in the night, he would eventually leave to go into his own room, so I was aware that I'd wake up alone. When I did, I realised it wasn't too difficult with him in just the next room. I got braver, and he promised to take me to see *Oliver Twist* at the Lowry theatre if I managed to sleep a full night alone. He knew my love of theatre, as he'd been the one to take me to am-dram groups from the age of three. It worked, and before I knew it, I was sitting in the dark auditorium, reaping my reward for being brave.

I ended up moving in with Dad a couple of times – for no longer than a fortnight at a time – as punishment for my unruly behaviour. On one occasion, I went into Preston to take my driving theory exam, failed it and returned home with a shiny new lip piercing instead. Mum and my stepdad hated tattoos and piercings. I'd already got my first tattoo on a high school trip to Germany when I was thirteen – it was supposed to be a star on my hip, but I winced so much with pain that the tattooist's hand kept slipping, so it ended up looking more like a wonky, wobbly pentagon. When I rocked through the door with a silver ball-bearing peering out of the bumfluff on my bottom lip, they hit the roof and shipped me off to live with Dad for two weeks. The second time was when I dropped out of Oxford. That one really hurt. I felt betrayed. I felt disposable, like a grain of sand in the desert, rather than a vital part of the family unit.

* * *

The experience of food on the farm was varied. My stepdad certainly encouraged us all to expand our palates. He'd always ask me to try something new from the menu in restaurants, and would wince a little if I asked for fillet steak, but kindly, he never said no. Not only did he want me to experience the excitement of food, I think he also hoped I would elevate myself from deep-fried Findus crispy pancakes, which my mum swears blind she never served us, but my sisters and I know she irrefutably did. I don't know why she protests so much, because they were delicious – crispy breadcrumbed batter housing a hot filling of some form of 'gravy'-soaked animal mince, what's not to love?

At farmers' markets, I'd ask for things like ostrich meat and crocodile, and my stepdad would be happy to oblige. I'll always be grateful to him for not minimising my experience of the culinary world. In many ways, food was, and still is, one of the only things I was free to explore when the thing I really needed to navigate was so disgusting.

Before my parents divorced, I remember the feeling of comfort around the dinner table. We'd laugh and joke as we ate the shepherd's pie and trifle that Mum had made. We called spaghetti 'spuz-getti', after my parents' Liverpudlian friend brought her son round and he asked for precisely that: 'I'll have spuz-getti, please!' But no such malapropisms or misnomers were allowed at the table on the farm. Our grammar was corrected, and my stepdad insisted that we ate with our knives and forks in the correct hands – something my sister Victoria struggled with.

Our dinnertimes had once been a way for our working-class family to be together, surrounded by love as we fulfilled one of the most basic human functions, refuelling, but now they transformed into middle-class conferences of control. Inappropriate jokes were stifled, conversation was formal and forced, unnatural and awkward. I don't blame my stepdad for this, not one bit. He had been sent to a private boarding school from a young age, so the use of the dinner table as a tool in navigating the class system was all he had known. And I feel deeply sorry for him in that regard. I wish he could have let himself experience the beauty of a raucous and rowdy feast. Perhaps, though, he derived his own comfort from the type of dinnertimes he insisted upon. There is, after all, more than one perspective in the multifarious experience of life with other people.

There's no doubt that I was a difficult child, so he certainly had his work cut out from the outset. I remember as we ate dinner in the garden one evening, I scooped out a heavy spoonful of ice cream and flicked it across the table, aiming for my sister. Never one for sports, my aim was completely off, and it hit my stepdad in the chest. My sisters and I fell to the floor, laughing, while my poor stepdad, embarrassed and covered in soft-scoop, withdrew my computer rights for a month.

As a child, I saw my stepdad as a wicked person – Mrs Trunchbull in male form. Only recently, when watching the stage adaptation of Neil Gaiman's *The Ocean at the End of the*

Lane, once more at the Lowry, did I come to appreciate that children think in magical and mystical ways, because that's their vocabulary. They're not able to process the perspective of all parties with empathy and understanding. But the emotions that drive both adult considerations and childhood illustrations are the same. As I've grown and experienced first-hand the sacrifices we all make in life, I have developed a deep gratitude towards him. In many ways, he is kind and loving. But when two worlds first collide, craters are inevitably left deep in the surface, and an understanding perspective from the adult I now am does nothing to help that scared little boy, lying cold on the floor outside his sisters' bedrooms.

★ ★ ★

One moment of great humour from those dinnertimes was Mum's inevitable fishing for compliments. My sisters and I still laugh about it now. Mum is a brilliant cook. Her food is rustic, well-seasoned and simply perfect. No matter how delicious it was, she'd apologise for it. 'I'm sorry everyone, it's a little underwhelming!' was a common statement, but the one that would have my sisters and I howling was: 'I've really let you all down here!'

Never once did any of her meals let us down – how could they have? We didn't always show our gratitude, but my God, what I'd give to have a meal cooked by my mum every night. I long for that sense of love. Bulimia didn't exist to me in those days, and keeping that food inside me was one of the only senses of safety I had.

Her crumbles never tickled my fancy, though. Is that putting it too politely? OK, they were crap. There was something about them that just turned my stomach – like the smell of overcooking Brussels sprouts on a Sunday afternoon after a visit to Grandma in the care home. The fruit was too watery and the crumble too fine, too powdery. I'd insist it was *all* crumble that I hated – perhaps out of sympathy for my mother, or perhaps due to a lack of experience – and it's only recently that I've tried a properly cooked crumble with a nuggety, crispy top. I like crumble now – adore it, in fact.

★ ★ ★

Despite the hard times, there were many happy memories on the farm, too. Our parties were the best. For Halloween, I'd spend weeks decorating the house with artificial cobwebs and skeletons – as if the house wasn't terrifying enough! My uncle Karl, a joiner, made us some wooden headstones for the garden. My stepdad would grumble, as I'd tilt all the artwork in the house at jaunty angles to make it look extra spooky, but by the time the party was underway, he was always in his element. When he allowed his inner child to gleam, it was beautiful to see. Now that my stepdad has grandchildren – my nephews – he allows that joy out even more.

Birthday parties were incredible. As a May baby, the sun always seemed to shine as my friends would hurl themselves around the bouncy castle or race around the fields. Someone would always inevitably trip and land in a fresh cowpat. I'd learned to avoid them. One year I started a new dance group late, so the role of Danny in *Grease* had already been allocated to a girlfriend of mine. Being the only lad in the dance troupe, I'd have automatically been given the role just weeks earlier. Luckily for me, but not so for her, she tumbled off the back of the bouncy castle and thrashed her ankle against the metal inflation pump. She ended up hobbling around in a plaster cast, while I joined the cast taking her role as the leading man. She took it well, and we'd laugh at how people might think I'd pushed her. But I wasn't even on the bouncy castle at the time of the event, My Lord.

Mum used to make vanilla traybakes covered in water icing. They were so simple – wonky and slightly caught in parts – yet the best birthday cakes a boy could wish for; though, admittedly, I did moan at her for not getting me a cake from 'Marks and Sparks'.

One year, my parents bundled me and about seven other children into the back of our old Land Rover and took us around Knowsley Safari Park. It started as a beautiful adventure – the tigers burned bright, the lions were fearsome – but it was the baboons that terrorised us. Windscreen wipers were torn from the vehicle, the rubber gaskets around the windows were pulled away. The gang of children in the back screamed in terror. I remember shouting, 'I should have brought my crucifix!' We taped the experience on a borrowed camcorder, but I can't find that VHS anywhere. I fear, out of embarrassment, I may have taped over it when filming myself as I performed Shania Twain's 'I'm Gonna Getcha Good' in a red wig I'd found in a puddle while out walking one day. Evidence of that, too, has been expunged from record.

It was in that same Land Rover that my stepdad taught me how to drive on the farm, long before I started to take professional lessons. First, I'd sit on his knee as we'd rattle around the fields, and I'd turn the wheel, clutching on to it tightly, not wanting to roll us over. But before long, I was in charge of the pedals, too. He was always kind and helpful in that way – maths homework, driving, changing wheels. He even showed me how to melt metal with a plumber's blowtorch and set it into shaped indentations in boxes of sand. I think that was his way of being kind, but looking back, maybe he was just trying to give me lead poisoning?

In baling season, we would all flock together in the fields, watching as the giant machines cut the straw then shaped and tied it into huge bricks. My sisters and I would wrestle with them, stacking them up on a trailer attached to a tractor. We'd work long into the night, when, chesty with hay fever and eyes stinging from the mix of allergy and exhaustion, we'd ride home on the top of the bales, in that long languishing dusk that summer nights bring. As the tractor trundled along the country roads, our heads would almost hit the branches of overhanging trees. My stepdad would shout back at us, 'Watch out for the hornets' nests!', which would make us dip and duck like action heroes. I loved it when the farmers worked late into the night during the harvest – from my bedroom window I could hear the roar and see the lights from their machines, and I didn't feel quite so alone.

★ ★ ★

There was a lot of hunting on the farm. At night, we'd all bundle into the Land Rover and head to the silage heap, which we illuminated with torches as my stepdad shot at the rats with an air rifle. I used to love that little bit of twisted fun, until Mum spoilt it by saying, 'The poor thing was on its way home from the shops with sweets for its little boy.' I never went ratting again after that. I'd imagine myself being shot at as I performed on stage, illuminated by the spotlights as I recited *Macbeth*.

I did go beating, though. At the weekends during the shooting season, I'd plough through the fields, streams and woodlands with a wooden stick one of the older beaters had formed and dried for me. I'd tap at tree trunks and disturb the grass to frighten the pheasants. They rocketed noisily into the sky, only to be plucked from flight by the ball bearings scattering from the farmers' shotguns.

If I wasn't on the shoot, I'd be helping Mum serve the shoot dinners. The hunters, in their tweed jackets and flat caps, rosy-cheeked from the bitter cold and the contents of their hipflasks, would joke and jibe, sometimes saying derogatory things about gays and gals. I ignored them – that was just who they were, and a little gobshite like me couldn't change their mindsets.

Although I was a night-time burden to my sisters, my God, were they protective of me! When my sister Jane moved into her own house and I stayed with her, she and Victoria would be the ones to confront the bullies who still plagued me at school. One night, after I returned to her house after a confrontation, they marched up fearlessly to the gang of lads and gave them a right royal bollocking. They could see how erosive the homophobia was. I wasn't out at that point, but I don't think it was a huge surprise when I did come out. In fact, I remember Jane coming into my room and telling me she didn't love me any less, and that I was still her little brother. My sisters were – and still are, to an extent – my lionesses.

Having people protect you, though, can be problematic in itself. Sometimes, they can go too far and you end up feeling responsible for their actions. I think that's especially true when it comes to sensitive subjects such as sexuality and gender. A few straight pals of mine have got into fights in my defence – some physical – and while that escalation was their decision, their choice, I can't help but feel responsible for those clouting conclusions. That, too, is something I've had to learn to let go of. We cannot control the choices of others. While I'm eternally grateful to have someone fighting my corner, I didn't pull the punches. Nor did I incite the hatred that led to the battle. I am not responsible for the actions of others.

★ ★ ★

Something I loved so much, and always looked forward to, was when Jane and I would go shopping together. We'd bat along to Southport or Wigan town centre in her convertible Smart car, singing Samantha Mumba or the *Beauty and the Beast* theme tune. She'd sometimes snap if I sang over her or came in at the wrong time and in the wrong key – she's certainly the epitome of a strong, independent woman. She once marched a roast chicken back to the shop because it was too lean, too meagre. She was about to unleash hell almighty on the poor, helpless shop worker, when she realised she had simply pulled the chicken out of the packet upside down and mistaken the scant backside for breast. Through working for Mum in the chippy, she managed to save up to buy her own house at just eighteen. What a girl!

One New Year's Eve, I was hosting a shop-bought dinner party at the farm for some college friends. As we meandered around the chilled section of Marks and Spencer's in Wigan, I declared, in a fairly loud voice: 'For dessert, I really want to serve, like, a chocolate flange.'

Jane turned crimson with embarrassment and immediately corrected me under her breath: 'John, it's chocolate FLAN!'

We were both horrified and amused in equal measure that I'd essentially told all of the grannies in 'Marks and Sparks' that what I longed for most was a chocolate vagina.

In the last year or two of high school, Mum sold the chippy and took over a dry-cleaning business half a mile down the road. On Saturdays, I'd work there with Jane for a few hours, washing clothes and accepting items for dry-cleaning. We'd sing together, as always. One day, Jane turned around and clocked me reciting, 'I wanna know what love is . . .' Unfortunately for me, I was holding the soiled nightie of a regular customer at the time – a rather unfriendly old lady. We laughed for days at me singing while tenderly clutching on to Mrs Smith's (not her real name) nightdress.

* * *

I came out, for a second time, to Mum in the dry-cleaner's. The first time was back in high school when a teacher I confided in phoned home, telling Mum I'd told her I was gay. After a few days of questions, I managed to climb back into the closet, and it wasn't mentioned again until this quiet Saturday, working with Mum. I was going through that insufferable moping stage that lovesick teenagers inflict upon themselves and every person with whom they come into contact. I was in love with a lad at college, but he wasn't interested. Like a sunflower, wherever he went, my head would turn, but it wasn't meant to be (thank God, I now think to myself!). I'd already had awkward conversations with Mum about the birds and the bees, after I'd slept with a girl for the first time. We did it in a field, and I was so out of my depth that when her eyes rolled back in her head and her breathing became fast and heavy, I offered to phone her an ambulance. We tumbled back, red-faced, with grass stains on our clothes. A few days later, Mum called me into her office and reminded me that even my *grandma* had had green smudges on her skirt.

Mum plucked up the courage to ask me outright, 'Darling, do you think you might be gay?'

I immediately broke down in tears and didn't have to answer. 'Are you mad at me?' I think I asked, eventually.

She reassured me that she'd love me no matter what. I was transported to my step-grandmother's wedding many years earlier, when a drunk family member had started to harass me for being 'effeminate'. So out of order was he, that even my sisters cried out of sympathy for me. Mum, like a wolf protecting its young, bared her teeth and hissed, 'I would *kill* for him!' When the shit hit the fan, I never questioned Mum's love for me.

She didn't want to tell my stepdad, though. I used to think it was because she was ashamed of me, and that my sexuality was a dirty secret, but I now know it was because she was protecting me. He had his opinions back then about homosexuality – opinions, I'm glad to say, that have changed. She knew there'd be an opportune moment to discuss it with him, and until then, she kept her cards close to her chest to protect her prince.

* * *

My mum and stepdad were both busy working – as well as running the chippy and then the dry-cleaner's, Mum worked in a nursing home, and also helped out with the dairy – so much of the time I was unsupervised on the farm. Alone, with a world of opportunity, I turned to what most teenage boys turn to: sex. The problem, though, is that my first major sexual experience was at the age of thirteen, with a man who was thirty. I consented and I wanted it, but in reality (and in law) a child cannot consent to sex with a person more than twice their age. For years, I thought nothing of it. But now, when I look at the innocence and youthfulness of my nephew, who is the age I was at the time, and I consider how I would react if I learned a grown man was doing the things to him that had been done to me, I dread to think how I would respond. He'd drive me down country lanes at night, unzip his trousers and ask me to perform oral sex on him as he slipped his hand down my hairless back and into me. If I learned the same was happening to my nephew, knuckles would be bloodied.

At the time, though, I was deeply ashamed of my sexuality,

which was becoming much more uncontainable and apparent to me – much harder to hide – and whenever I confided in this man, I felt accepted. I felt loved. Time with him was a tonic to the loneliness I felt: the geographical remoteness of the farm coupled with my feeling of being emotionally outcast because of my sexuality. Like a fox homes in on an injured sheep, he had me in his sights. I started to confuse a feeling of being loved with a sexual openness that has been difficult to overcome. Ever since, I haven't respected my body in a way that I should. I've been too willing to let people have pieces of me that would have been better retained and reserved for someone who showed me respect and kindness.

My experiences with male role models would definitely have an impact on many of my future relationships with men – not just sexual relationships, but platonic ones, too. My stepdad had been my teacher, yet, in a way, was somewhat oppressive and authoritarian. My dad was a source of great comfort, but time with him was sometimes used as a punishment. And the thirty-year-old man appeared to be a confidant, while taking advantage of my isolation and the fear I had of my sexuality.

Mum had already taught me about the inescapable certainty of death. But life experience expands on that. Because it isn't just the death of the living body we need to fear. It is the death of our youth, the loss of our innocence, that serves to torment us. It is the devastating realisation that not all forms of love add to who we are as a person. Some subtract. Some are merely illusions that leave us bereft and in agony for something that never even was, never could have been. That isn't something you can just bury and forget.

But who knows what's waiting when you turn a different corner?

Rhubarb and Apple Crumble

————

SERVES 6–8

A crumble was always my least favourite bake of Mum's. I don't know how she did them, but the fruit was always too watery and the crumble too sandy and powdery; if you inhaled too deeply with a spoonful of crumble close by, it could have been lethal. Despite my hyperbole, they weren't *terrible*, and I'd probably almost enjoy one nowadays. But the way each of us likes our crumble is deeply personal. I can cope with a dry bit of cake or a claggy scone, but a crumble that isn't golden brown, nuggety and crispy just isn't worth the energy required to eat it – that's why I'd never order a crumble off a restaurant menu without it coming fully recommended by someone I trust. I like my crumble with the fruit just cooked, with a slight bite. It should be sweet enough, but not sickly sweet, and the topping – the most important part – should be a mixture of the finer sand Mum's was littered with (sorry, Mum!) and coarser, nuggety chunks. I also think it should take reference from a proper crème brûlée; there should be a bite of topping in every spoonful, so I make it fairly shallow in its fruit layer, meaning that with every bite, there's crumble. If you like a deeper pool of fruit with just a dusting of crumble, bake it in a 23cm (9in) round pie dish and halve the quantities for the crumble topping itself.

This is just how I like it – whatever is good for you, great. That's the beauty of being just one of eight billion people on Earth – there's certainly a lot of variety around.

75g (2⅔) caster (superfine) sugar
1 tablespoon custard powder (like Bird's)
¼ teaspoon ground cinnamon
¼ teaspoon ground ginger
¼ teaspoon ground nutmeg
pinch of ground cloves
4 large Cox apples (about 550g/1lb 4oz)
400g (14oz) rhubarb

For the crumble topping
200g (7oz) plain (all-purpose) flour
150g (5½oz) unsalted butter
100g (3½oz) light brown muscovado sugar

- Preheat the oven to 200°C/180°C fan/400°F/gas mark 6.

- Put the sugar, custard powder and spices into a large mixing bowl and whisk together until evenly combined. Peel, core and dice three of the apples into roughly 2cm (1in) chunks – some can be a little larger, if that's what you fancy. Coarsely grate the fourth apple, then add them all to the mixing bowl. Cut half of the rhubarb into 1cm (½in) chunks, and the rest into 3cm (1¼in) chunks, and add to the bowl. Toss the fruit with the sugar mixture until evenly coated, then tip into a roasting dish – mine is about 23cm (9in) square.

- For the crumble topping, put all the ingredients into a food processor and blitz to a mealy sand consistency. Remove a quarter of it and set it aside, then continue processing the rest until it starts to clump together into a damp, nugget consistency – rather like granola. Mix the coarser, nuggety crumble in with the sandy stuff, then scatter evenly over the fruit.

- Bake for 35–40 minutes, or until the crumble is golden brown – perhaps even a little caught in places, if you like it that way. Remove from the oven and allow to cool slightly, then serve with custard, cream or ice cream – or all three, if that's what you need.

Birthday Cake Slab

—————

SERVES 12–16

This is 'inspired by' rather than an actual re-creation of the birthday slab cakes Mum would make when I was little. For a start, she would have most likely stuck with a classic Victoria sponge recipe, which she'd scale up and bake in a bigger tin. Hers were also often a little caught at the edges, which I'm hoping the below will not be for you. But I think the biggest diversion from tradition here, beyond the inclusion of buttermilk, is the reverse creaming method. Beating the fat into the dry ingredients before adding the milk and eggs reduces the amount of gluten produced during the mixing process. It makes for a much lighter sponge. This cake lends itself well to almost any topping, so I've listed three below: chocolate ganache, cream cheese and a lemon drizzle.

225g (8oz) Stork baking spread or margarine,
plus extra for greasing
300g (10½oz) caster (superfine) sugar
340g (12oz) self-raising flour
1 teaspoon baking powder
½ teaspoon fine salt
4 large eggs

1 tablespoon vanilla bean paste
250ml (9oz) buttermilk

- Preheat the oven to 180°C/160°C fan/350°F/gas mark 4. Grease a 23 × 33cm (9 × 13in) baking tin and line with baking paper (parchment paper).

- In a mixing bowl, beat the baking spread, sugar, flour, baking powder and salt with a handheld electric whisk until you have a thick paste. In a separate bowl, whisk together the eggs, vanilla and buttermilk, then gradually add this mixture to the paste mixture, beating as you go. Beat just until you have a smooth batter – don't overmix it, or it will become tough as it bakes.

- Pour the batter into the prepared tin, spread level with a spoon or small offset spatula, then bake for 30–40 minutes, or until a skewer inserted into the centre of the cake comes out clean. Allow the cake to cool completely in the tin before lifting it out and applying the topping. The cake, with any of the topping options below, will keep in an airtight container for 4 days. You could also freeze the cake – I'd place it on a baking sheet and freeze it for an hour, then wrap it in clingfilm (plastic wrap) and return it to the freezer where it will keep for 3 months.

Topping Options

Chocolate Ganache Buttercream

This is a hybrid of chocolate ganache and buttercream. It makes for a chocolate buttercream that is neither sickly sweet nor overly dark, and the aeration of the buttercream means the ganache is lightened beyond belief.

150g (5½oz) double (heavy) cream
150g (5½oz) dark chocolate (60 per cent cocoa solids),
roughly chopped
100g (3½oz) unsalted butter
200g (7oz) icing (confectioners') sugar
sprinkles, to decorate

- Put the cream and chocolate into a heatproof bowl and set over a pan of barely simmering water. Stirring occasionally, allow the chocolate to melt into the cream. Once the mixture is smooth and glossy, remove from the heat and allow to cool until thick – it should be the consistency of Nutella.

- Put the butter and icing sugar into a separate bowl and whisk together (starting off gently to avoid a huge cloud of icing sugar in the air) until pale and fluffy. Add the chocolate cream mixture and whisk until you have a smooth, velvety buttercream. Spread the buttercream over the cooled cake and finish with sprinkles.

Cream Cheese Frosting

A sweet but sharp cream cheese frosting has to be one of my favourites. I'd never make this in a stand mixer, as they are far too powerful and can make the frosting very slack. Instead, I use a handheld electric mixer. Please don't be tempted to use anything other than full-fat cream cheese; if you do, it won't hold and you'll be sorry (not a threat, just a fact).

150g (5½oz) unsalted butter, at room temperature
150g (5½oz) icing (confectioners') sugar, sifted
300g (11oz) full-fat cream cheese, fridge-cold
sprinkles, to decorate

- In a large bowl, beat the butter and icing sugar together until pale and fluffy. I find it useful to start beating them together with a wooden spoon, to avoid an almighty dust cloud, then switch to the handheld electric mixer. Once fluffy, add the cream cheese and beat in just until smooth. Spread over the cooled cake and finish with sprinkles.

Lemon Drizzle and Water Icing

This topping is much closer to what Mum would make, though I don't think she would have made it lemon-flavoured, because that wouldn't have gone so well with the Freddo bars that she would place around the edges of the cake.

For the drizzle
75ml (5 tablespoons) fresh lemon juice
60g (2¼oz) caster (superfine) sugar

For the icing
250g (9oz) icing (confectioners') sugar
zest and juice of 1 lemon

- Once the cake has cooled, poke it repeatedly with a skewer to create little holes for the drizzle to soak into.

- To make the drizzle, combine the lemon juice and sugar in a small saucepan over a high heat and bring to the boil, then remove from the heat and pour over the cooled cake. Allow to cool.

- For the icing, mix the icing sugar with 1 tablespoon of the lemon juice in a bowl, adding more as needed, a drop at a time, until you have a thickly flowing water icing. Drizzle it over the cake, spread out as needed, then finish with the lemon zest.

Chocolate and Biscoff Flan(ge)

————

SERVES 8

If I could have described the perfect chocolate *'flange'* on that day of my embarrassing Marks & Spencer malapropism, this would have been it. I created this recipe only very recently for a supermarket client, but it's precisely what I was wanting to serve at my New Year's dinner party some eighteen years ago.

For the base
40g (1½oz) unsalted butter
25g (1oz) dark chocolate
25g (1oz) milk chocolate
200g (7oz) bourbon biscuits or Oreos,
plus extra to decorate (optional)

For the filling
100g (3½oz) Biscoff spread (cookie butter)

For the topping
125g (4½oz) dark chocolate, roughly chopped
125g (4½oz) milk chocolate, roughly chopped,
plus about 75g (2⅔oz) extra to decorate (optional)
50g (2oz) unsalted butter

2 large eggs

30g (1oz) caster (superfine) sugar

- For the base, melt together the butter and the dark and milk chocolates in a heatproof bowl set over a pan of simmering water, stirring to combine.

- Meanwhile, crush the bourbon biscuits to fine crumbs – either bash with a rolling pin or whizz them in a food processor – and tip into a bowl. Once the chocolate mixture has melted, pour it over the biscuit crumbs and stir until well combined.

- Tip the mixture into a 20cm (8in) fluted tart tin and press into the base and sides as evenly as possible. Chill, covered, for 20 minutes.

- Spread the Biscoff spread on to the cooled biscuit shell, then cover and return to the fridge while you make the chocolate topping.

- For the topping, melt the dark and milk chocolates with the butter in a large heatproof bowl set over a pan of simmering water. Once melted, remove from the heat and set aside. In another large heatproof bowl, whisk the eggs and sugar over a pan of simmering water. Don't stop whisking as the bowl heats up, or the eggs will coagulate, and you'll need to start again.

- Once the egg mixture is loose and feels hot to the touch (this will take about 5 minutes), pour it into the melted chocolate mixture and whisk to a smooth, silky ganache. Pour this topping into the tart case, then chill for about 2 hours until set. This will keep for 4 days in the fridge.

- The tart looks impressive as it is, but if you want to decorate it, melt the extra milk chocolate in a bowl set over a pan of simmering water, then use a spoon to drizzle it around the edge of the tart. Scatter over some crumbled bourbon or Oreo biscuits.

Coffee and Pecan Traybake

———

SERVES 12–16

Even to this day, if Mum throws a party of some sort, she'll ask me to contribute to the cake spread – and without any doubt, she will ask for her favourite coffee and walnut or pecan. She'll insist I make more than even double the number of guests in attendance could get through, so her freezer is always stashed with coffee and pecan cake slices.

For the cake
280g (10oz) Stork baking spread (or margarine),
plus extra for greasing
280g (10oz) caster (superfine) sugar
280g (10oz) self-raising flour
2 teaspoons baking powder
½ teaspoon fine salt
5 large eggs
125g (4½oz) pecans, toasted and roughly chopped
2 tablespoons instant coffee granules dissolved in
3 tablespoons warm milk

For the syrup
100g (3½oz) dark brown muscovado sugar

100ml (3½fl oz) water
1 tablespoon instant coffee granules

For the frosting and to decorate
1 × batch Cream Cheese Frosting (page 70, but see note on page 77)
2 tablespoons instant coffee granules dissolved in
2 tablespoons warm milk
100g (3½oz) pecans, toasted and roughly chopped
100g (3½oz) dark chocolate (70 per cent cocoa solids),
roughly chopped

- Preheat the oven to 180°C/160°C fan/350°F/gas mark 4. Grease a 23 × 33cm (9 × 13in) baking tray and line with baking paper (parchment paper).

- First make the cake. In a stand mixer, mix together the baking spread, caster sugar, flour, baking powder and salt until you have a thick paste. Beat the eggs in a small jug, then slowly incorporate them into the paste as you beat on a medium speed. Once you have a smooth batter, fold in the pecans, then marble in the dissolved coffee – you don't want this to be fully incorporated, but instead running in thick, dark streaks through the batter. Scoop the batter into the prepared tin, level off, then bake for 25–40 minutes, or until a skewer inserted into the centre of the cake comes out clean.

- Meanwhile, make the syrup. Simply bring the sugar, water and coffee granules to the boil in a small saucepan over a high heat. Once the cake has baked, stab it repeatedly with a skewer, then pour the syrup over the top.

- Make the frosting according to the method on page 70, but before you add the cream cheese, beat the dissolved coffee granules into the butter and icing sugar, then proceed as detailed. Spread the frosting over the cooled, soaked cake, before sprinkling over the chopped pecans and chocolate. This will keep for 4 days in an airtight container.

Spiced Pineapple Traybake

———

SERVES 12–16

This is a more recent evolution from the traybakes that have always appeared at birthdays or parties on the farm. It's a recipe I created for my sister, Our Vic, for her fortieth birthday, and it really did go down a storm.

For the cake
150ml (5fl oz) sunflower oil, plus extra for greasing
435g (15¼oz) can pineapple slices in juice
3 large eggs
375g (13oz) caster (superfine) sugar
270g (9½oz) plain (all-purpose) flour
65g (2¼oz) desiccated (dried shredded) coconut
1½ teaspoons bicarbonate of soda (baking soda)
1 teaspoon fine salt
1 teaspoon ground cinnamon
1 teaspoon ground ginger
½ teaspoon ground nutmeg
½ teaspoon ground cloves

For the frosting and to top
1 × batch Cream Cheese Frosting (page 70)

small handful of dried pineapple pieces
small handful of coconut chips

- Preheat the oven to 180°C/160°C fan/350°F/gas mark 4. Grease a 23 × 33cm (9 × 13in) baking tin and line with baking paper (parchment paper).

- To make the cake, blitz the pineapple slices and their juice in a blender or food processor until you have a purée. Pour this into a bowl and mix in the oil and eggs.

- In a separate bowl, whisk together the sugar, flour, coconut, bicarbonate of soda, salt and spices, then add the wet ingredients and beat just until smoothly combined – don't overmix. Pour into the prepared cake tin and bake for 30–35 minutes. Allow to cool completely in the tin, before lifting out to decorate.

- Spread the cream cheese frosting over the cooled cake, then scatter over the pineapple pieces and coconut chips.

3.
Hotel Carpet Picnics

I wasn't particularly afraid of growing up camp. My dad, after all, wasn't the manliest of men you could have met. A musician and actor with an amateur dramatics group, he was born to perform. If he wasn't doing somersaults in the sack race at my sports day, he was in his music room singing at the top of his lungs, accompanying himself on the piano. In my later years of high school, he and some mates of his formed a rock 'n' roll band, which would tour the Lancashire club circuit most weekends. I was their roadie, so would ride in the back of the van with the drummer, help unload the kit and sit at the bar as they clicked into the microphones, testing levels. When the night was in full swing and they played songs like 'Hotel California' and 'Witchy Woman', I'd thrash around the dancefloor with girls, twisting to the ground on the balls of my feet and peacocking freely.

I'd sometimes wait around the toilets, hoping a lad might

want to chat to me, make me do things to him like the thirty-year-old had. I wanted more of that. It had lit a fire inside of me. But thankfully, no one ever paid me an ounce of attention in that way.

It wasn't campness that I feared, but rejection and loneliness, and that had frightened me since long before these nights on the dancefloors of these run-down clubs.

I was in McDonald's in Chorley when I first panicked about being alone for ever. I can't have been more than eight. After my parents split up, Dad would take us for a Happy Meal and a walk most Sundays. That day, I stood beside him and watched a man order his lunch. His voice was soft, his hair well-groomed and his eyebrows tweezed into barely visible thin strips. He reminded me a lot of Dale Winton (a name, coincidentally, bullies in high school would call me), and I panicked. I didn't want to grow up to be like him – alone. I don't know how I'd come to the conclusion that this man must be lonely. Perhaps it was because he stood out, coupled with the fact that he was alone that day, but I remember him conveying a sense of being guarded, as though he was ready to flee in the face of conflict, as though he was on edge. Even as he sat eating his Big Mac, he had an air of sadness about him.

I was certain that's how I would end up: alone. I was sure I would become a hermit in the local village, whispered about in hushed tones, rather like a great-uncle of ours, whose sexuality we never spoke about. He'd never married, and, rejected by some of his siblings, he lived on the edge of the village.

Whenever I'd visit him – usually at Halloween, because he'd make jack-o'-lanterns from small pumpkins, with marbles for eyeballs – I always assumed he was alone.

Children's books in school focused on Mummy and Daddy, and their two-point-four children and their doggy and their wonderful happy life with a yellow bloody sun in the bright-blue sky. There was never a mention of the outcasts. Gay kisses in soap operas were scandalous – even salacious – and warranted an abrupt changing of the channel in many homes. At family weddings, the priest would harp on about how marriage was a bond between man and woman. Couples holding hands in the street were of the opposite sex. Everything I was feeling inside me was demonised by scripture and media – or at least those to which I had access. Everything I was feeling was, therefore, fearsome.

By the time George Michael was arrested by the police in the USA and forced to come out in 1998, he'd already been subjected to multiple outing attempts at the hands of the rabid tabloid press – interviewers would broach the topic, but he'd always so graciously deflect. It was his story, his reality, his identity. It was *his* life. But the media dehumanised him. When those events in California unfolded, I watched the reactions of my school peers and family friends. These reactions horrified me. It was as though people would only accept his overt showmanship if they too were in on the joke, if it was sweet and digestible. They made me want to become that hermit, there and then. To recede into the shadows.

When you consider that homophobia was rife within the statute book as well as society at large, it isn't difficult to understand how hatred has been perpetuated and fuelled within the UK and monetised by the press. Homosexuality was illegal until 1967, but in 1988, under Thatcher's government, the infamous Section 28 of the Local Government Act further gripped the reins of exclusion. With the bold aim of 'prohibiting the promotion of homosexuality', the legislation ensured no talk of same-sex relationships or character depictions were allowed in local authorities or schools – no books, no films, no scripts in which gay people were represented could be part of classroom discussion. Teachers who broke the law would face disciplinary action. Attempts were made to wipe gay people from history before they could even be a part of it. And on top of this, the fact that the devastation of the HIV/AIDS pandemic was framed as a 'gay disease' further sustained hatred.

But queer people didn't roll over and accept this attempt at erasing them. On 20 February 1988, over 20,000 people protested in the streets of Manchester, despite growing police hostility towards the LGBTQ+ community. Lesbians stormed a BBC newsroom in May that year. The queer world was aflame, fuelled by rage, propelled by the desire to simply have the freedom to exist, safely.

Section 28 was only repealed in November 2003. But in some people, the mindset of homophobia lived on – it didn't need to be enshrined in law to be felt.

★ ★ ★

At college, after I came out, I was at ease for a while. My friends and tutors were all aware of my sexuality, and it was accepted – celebrated, even. I immersed myself in every college performance I could – happy to play the role of a car-park attendant, if that was all there was. I always thought of my Shakespeare drama teacher, Christine, whose mantra was: 'There are no small parts, only small actors.' Even to this day, when I start to get a little big for my boots and wish for a larger role in whatever I'm working on, I say those words to myself. They plonk my feet back on *terra firma*. Theatre had been my first love. The applause and acceptance it offered sort of numbed the naysaying and judgement.

Although I was academically bright and enjoyed all my subjects – Spanish, French and philosophy and religion – I loved drama the most. I really wanted to go to drama school, to do a degree in musical theatre or drama. I got a call back to the Guildford School of Acting, but Mum and my stepdad were keen to remind me that it was a 'saturated market' and that there were better people out there. They weren't wrong, because it *is* a saturated market, but *most* markets are saturated. If you're going to fight to get a seat at an already crowded table, shouldn't it be one that you truly want to sit at in the first place? They were frightened for my future, for my security, I get that. I see their perspective. But you can't wrap someone in cotton wool for ever. There's a danger in dampening someone's soul and extinguishing the fires within their heart; it can leave them with nothing but ashes where they once burned.

I tried to fight back, but eventually gave in and applied to read medieval and modern languages at St John's College at Oxford University. I only applied to that particular college because I had the highest chance of getting in based on its application-to-admission ratio. I applied with a nonchalance, a kind of hope that I would be rejected, but it seems fate had other plans.

I was invited to go down for an interview. My mum and stepdad drove me down the night before, and we ate Italian food together. I had dyed a blond patch in the front of my hair – a mudflap, my sister called it – and they nagged at me over dinner, telling me how daft it looked, worrying that the university wouldn't let me in with such a silly hairdo. It made me want to abandon my plate of pasta and rush to a salon, rifle through the hair dye cupboard and make myself look like a multicoloured skunk – anything for the university to reject me. But it seems even Oxford academics aren't quite the stiff conservatives my parents had anticipated; they looked past my jazzy hairdo.

Whatever they might have thought of my hair, I did have a feeling that I was completely inferior and shouldn't have even been there. I didn't think of myself as being particularly clever – I was just lucky I had a good memory and could digest and regurgitate bucketloads of information: some useful, some not so useful.

I sat, nervously, in the office of Dr Emanuela Tandello, tutor in Italian, which was over in a different college – Christ Church. The room was dimly lit and cosy, full of bookshelves. I sat, with my silly hairdo, on the sofa. Dr Tandello sat facing me, her back to the window. She had a friendly, smiling face – she looked rather like Isabella Rossellini. She was encouraging. She asked me to read a poem, 'Crossing the Water' by Sylvia Plath. She asked what it reminded me of, and the Greek myth of Orpheus and Eurydice came to mind – one I had been obsessed with when learning about Greek mythology way back in primary school. On their wedding day, Eurydice was killed by a poisonous snake and her soul was taken to the Underworld. Her husband, Orpheus, bravely headed there, crossing the river Styx, to retrieve her from Hades, the god of the dead, and bring her back to the mortal realms. It was just a dramatic version of all the love stories I'd seen on *Coronation Street* and *Emmerdale*; though, I'm not quite sure Diedre Rashid would have crossed a river of lost souls to save Ken Barlow. I wondered if I'd ever feel that compelled to make such a sacrifice for another person; would I ever be that lucky?

I left feeling a certain smugness. Not because I felt clever, but because despite my hair, the thing my parents had harped on about all through dinner, this lovely, smiling, encouraging Italian tutor had seen past my aesthetic choices and was more interested in what I had to say, based on the experiences I'd had, the books I'd read, the movies I'd watched. I felt like shouting a big 'fuck you' to the teacher in high school who had called me a poof when I'd dyed my hair in that checkerboard pattern. Perhaps I muttered the words into the leaf-littered wind as I wound my way out of the labyrinthine halls.

★ ★ ★

Within weeks, a big, fat letter arrived from the university, which my stepdad opened (with my permission) while I was at college. I received an offer, conditional on three A grades at A level. My friends in the performing arts block all cheered, but my heart sank. I cried to my drama teacher, told her I didn't want to go. The college therapist suggested I write a letter to my parents, explaining that I wasn't ready to go to Oxford, but nothing worked. I knew I had to give it a try. I knew, more certainly, that it wasn't going to work out well – the thread of my future had already been spun.

My mum and stepdad drove me down to Oxford the Sunday before my course was due to start. George Michael's episode of *Desert Island Discs* came on the radio, and I listened intently. He spoke candidly about the contrasting events of his year: opening his tour in front of thousands at Wembley Stadium the day after appearing in the dock before the magistrate at Brent charged with driving under the influence. He spoke about his patriarchal upbringing, and how the male child was always fawned over and came first. I thought of my sisters; neither of them went to university. Jane's education was probably disrupted by the divorce and the fact that she worked with Mum in the chippy, and Our Vic was a wild child; though, she did work extremely hard in her hairdressing career. She just seemed less bothered by the constraints of the future. Being both the youngest and the only boy of my full siblings, I had certainly been given more time and attention. I felt guilty for that, just like George did. My sisters would call me 'golden boy', but they didn't see how debilitating it was; I sometimes felt like a performing monkey.

I didn't ever settle in at Oxford. I felt like an outsider. Don't get me wrong, I made some really strong friendships – one of whom, Concepta, I'm still in contact with – but there was an air of privilege there that I'd never experienced. The children of businessmen, politicians and foreign diplomats would laugh and joke in the quads. It was all so posh, so exclusive – and, from the perspective of a farmer's son from Wigan, so wanky.

It wasn't just the social imbalance that made me feel uneasy it was the drink and drugs culture, too. Oxford was the last place I'd expected to be so hedonistic, but it was. We drank most nights – if not at a weekend bop (like a school disco), it was weeknights in the bar. Cocaine was fairly commonplace, too. One girl, a medical student, as far as I can remember, had a computer unit that was just a façade, behind which were hidden bags of white powder which she'd distribute to whoever wanted some.

I knew I needed to get out of there – not just because I felt inadequate, but because the temptation was too strong. If I drank every night, if I got started on the coke, I knew I'd become unstable.

The straw that broke the camel's back, though, was a word. I was sitting in a seminar with Dr Tandello and other students, discussing Primo Levi's holocaust memoir *Se questo è un uomo* (*If This Is a Man*). One student used the word 'succinct', and I felt a tingle of shame wash over my body because I didn't understand its meaning. In that brief moment, I decided I would defer for a year. Dr Tandello understood. She took me to the Randolph Hotel for tea and shortbread and told me it was normal to not feel ready. I'd shaved my hair by this point.

She didn't comment on that. She just wanted to make sure I was OK.

My dad had to come and get me, because Mum and my stepdad were furious that I was giving up after just six weeks. I moved in with Dad for a little while, because it was as though they couldn't even stand to look at me. I felt the weight of failure on my shoulders. I felt that if I didn't perform to their script, I didn't have a part. If I didn't live up to their standards of success, I was unsuccessful. For the winter, I got a part-time job in Selfridges, Manchester, working for a perfume company. I was able to fit in there, wearing light make-up like the other lads and a skintight all-black uniform. It wasn't a place of judgement.

The following summer, I tried to brush up on my Italian, so that I'd be ready to return to Oxford in the autumn. I went to Rome for a month – my mum and stepdad paid for the trip, desperate for a secure future for me – then got a job in the Milan office of the perfume manufacturer I'd worked for in Selfridges, and stayed there for another month. By the time the summer was over, my Italian was just as strong as my Spanish, and I felt linguistically ready to return to Oxford. Deep down, though, I remained totally uninterested in studying there and dreaded going back.

★ ★ ★

Towards the end of that summer, I met Paul. On Facebook, before the days of Grindr, Tinder and other apps of instant gratification (if you're lucky), there was an application called 'Are You Interested?'. Random profile pictures from within a certain radius would pop up, and you'd simply click 'yes' or 'no'. Paul popped up, handsome like Ryan Reynolds, with a lovely smile. We got chatting. I can't remember what our first conversation was like – I dread to think – but we ended up arranging a date.

When the day of the date came, I was working with my brother-in-law, who was renovating a house. I got cold feet and told Paul I had diarrhoea and had to cancel, but my brother-in-law told me I was being silly and that I should just go. 'If it works out, great; if it doesn't, then at least you have a nice night and meal out.' His words carried so much weight, because he was a straight man. I naturally expected straight men to make it into a joke '. . . at least you'll meet a new bum chum!', but he didn't. He supported me.

I had a word with myself, messaged Paul to say I was feeling better and headed into Manchester.

I turned the corner from Shudehill on to Thomas Street in Manchester's trendy Northern Quarter, and there he was. Tall (half an inch taller than me) and so bloody handsome. He smiled at me, then waved. I couldn't believe how gorgeous he was. We walked to Simple on Tib Street and sat for hours. Some parts of the conversation I remember, some I don't, but what I do remember without any doubt is that we laughed.

When I'm nervous, I eat; when Paul is nervous, he cannot. He was shocked at just how much I put away – plate after plate arrived at our table, and I pretty much sank the lot. After dinner, we walked over to Canal Street, where my dad was with his mates. I introduced Paul to my dad, and they got on well. Dad used to take me to Canal Street a lot while I was in college. My first Gay Pride, in fact, was with him. I wore bright-red trousers, an acid-green T-shirt and pink braces. We sat in a quiet pub on the boundary of the gay village as I plucked up courage to talk to strangers in the scattering light of the glitterball, just as he had encouraged me to get on the karaoke stage at the Ocean Edge caravan park in Heysham, the best part of a decade before.

At the end of the date, Paul walked me to my car. Embarrassingly, my Solo bank card wouldn't work on the paying machine – I'd spent my last £20 on dinner. Paul had to pay for my parking. I thanked him with a quick peck on the lips. I thought about that kiss the whole way home. When I got back, I made meatballs and sent him a picture with the caption 'I'm still hungry.' I didn't sleep that night, not because I was excited, but because I was worried. I liked what I saw in Paul, I was hugely attracted to him, and he seemed to be a man of values – family came first for him. I knew it because of the way his eyes sparkled when he spoke of them. I was afraid that we might turn into nothing, that maybe this was me merely brushing shoulders with someone on my journey to ultimate loneliness.

But I proved my fears wrong, as I found myself eating fish-finger sandwiches on our second date, and, after a pint of beer, sharing a good old-fashioned sloppy snog in a cocktail bar. I felt safe with him. Not in an overly romanticised or projected way; he just had a calmness about him, a self-possessed quality.

Over the next few weeks, we went on more and more dates: the cinema, the canteen at Ikea for meatballs, failed walks in Grizedale Forest that turned into boat trips on Grasmere lake.

The more we got to know each other, the more we fell for one another. He met my mum, in the same bar where we'd had our first date. She seemed to really like him, but didn't fail to labour the point that I was to return to Oxford in the autumn, and that Paul was to make sure I went and stayed there. We didn't tell my stepdad about him just yet; it wasn't worth the hassle.

I didn't meet Paul's family for at least nine months. Afraid of the rejection that was all too commonplace within the queer community, he hadn't yet come out to them. There were a couple of close calls. Once, while out shopping, we bumped into his eldest sister, who looked at me knowingly and smiled with the same love-filled eyes that Paul has. I knew from that look, despite never having met the rest of his family, that they knew.

★ ★ ★

October came and I was shipped off to Oxford again, but I had no intention of staying there. I was in love. We hadn't shared those three words yet, but I knew we felt them. When the time came, as we chatted over the phone, I curled up on my bed in my room, dying to say 'I love you', but I was too nervous. My stomach was like a pit of butterflies, all high on caffeine and jelly babies, desperate to unleash themselves on the world. I'd told an ex-boyfriend I loved him, but that paled in comparison to this. That was lust – ownership, perhaps – but this was something else; this was oxygen and nourishment. It was a desperate and urgent need to be there, to learn about each other, to battle through life together. I quietly uttered the words. He fell silent, then, almost with a sigh of relief replied, 'I love you too.'

Paul came to pick up me and my belongings the second and last time I dropped out of Oxford. My mum and stepdad were away, so he helped me unpack and stayed the night. Despite Mum's harsh words the first time he'd met her, those warnings to keep me at university, he'd boldly ignored them. He could see what was best for me and followed that path. Paul is the kind of guy who would humbly tell you he is soft, a scaredy-cat. But, guided by his morals and principles, he is fearless.

When we told my stepdad about our relationship, he seemed to instantly like Paul – everyone does. But his rules were strict: no sleepovers. I didn't fight back. It wasn't worth it, and it was *his* house after all. That's the problem with step-parents sometimes. They can be territorial. It never felt like *our* home as a family, it always felt like *his*. It still does, in a way.

So, we'd spend weekend nights in the cheapest hotels we could find, and we loved it. We'd gather hoards of snacks from Marks and Spencer: bottles of prosecco, pork pies, Scotch eggs and, of course, bags of Percy Pigs. We'd eat these picnics as we snuggled on the hotel rooms' threadbare carpets, watching *The X Factor* or films. It didn't matter that the location became more ramshackle each week, because our love became more polished. Together, we were home. When we *were* finally allowed to sleep over, we were in separate rooms. But what my stepdad forgot was that there was a crawl space between my room and the spare room, put there for building regulations. One of us would lock the door and drag ourselves through the dusty hole, then snuggle down together and crawl back at first light.

★ ★ ★

When out and about, we had to carefully analyse a setting before we could decide whether or not it was safe to hold hands. People shouting homophobic slurs had become boring and tiresome. In the cinema, we'd need to be on guard if I wanted to lean my head on his shoulder: a quick scan around the auditorium first. On the escalator in Next, we were holding hands and laughing with one another. A woman, coming down in the opposite direction, smiled brightly, held up her thumb and said, 'Good for you, lads!'

It seemed that for each troll lurking under a bridge, there was at least one cheerleader.

After being together for a while, I could see the pain it was causing Paul to still be in the closet. He wanted to tell his family, but didn't know how or when. I told him that if he couldn't do it, then perhaps we couldn't be together. It was risky, I know, but his friends kept telling him to do it, and after seeing the knowing smile his sister had given me while shopping that day, I just knew it would be OK.

And it was.

He told them the morning after our conversation, and that night I was at their house, meeting them for the first time. It was wrong of me, though, to control the narrative in that way. It was *his* life, *his* family. If they had rejected him, I wouldn't have suffered the consequences. I feel guilty about that. Thankfully, the best possible outcome unfolded, but one of the dangers of young love is that it can be selfish and impulsive.

Paul's dad was the first person I met that evening. He stood up excitedly, maybe also nervously, shook my hand and winked at me. He was instantly warm and welcoming, just like Paul had been on our first date. His mum was upstairs making the bed, so up I went. She was friendly, too, and we chatted as she did the ironing about what I did for a living. By that time, I was working for the Co-operative Insurance Services, modifying car insurance policies over the phone. It was a dull job, repetitive and mundane, but it put money in my pocket and kept me out of the house. The conversation soon turned to food, and somehow, we got to chatting about corned beef hash. That's Paul's favourite food on the planet. Nothing I could ever make will compare with his mother's corned beef hash.

Pretty soon, I'd met his entire family. Most weekends, we'd be at his family home – which very much reminded me of the house I'd lived in before Mum and Dad divorced – where we'd spend entire afternoons together, eating, drinking and laughing. My own family felt fairly fragmented in comparison. The only time we ever got together was for bigger events, such as Christmas and Easter, but they weren't relaxed and easy like this. They were formal: the ridiculously long table in the oak-framed dining room, often arranged to a seating plan devised by my stepdad. That constraint was the exact opposite of the flowing, endless freedom I felt with Paul's family. On those afternoons, it felt as though the sun would never descend, and that we could laugh together for ever.

They loved a film, Paul's family, so we'd often cram together in the living room, almost on top of each other, as we sipped cans of lager and bottles of wine. One of the first films we watched together – *The Bank Job* with Jason Statham, I think – opened with a throbbing sex scene. I could feel my cheeks burning scarlet with embarrassment, so I quietly slipped away and raced home in my mum's Smart car. I wasn't quite ready to be *that* comfortable with my new in-laws.

Equally embarrassing was the time we all played football in the field opposite the house. I'd never liked ball games, especially not after my stepdad thought it would be a good idea to sign me up for rugby. The only match I ever played was a disaster. I didn't understand the rules, so when I grabbed the ball, I just kept running, flinging lads off me and crying underneath my helmet. The referees were whistling, and people were shouting at me to stop, but I just kept running. I was being held back by a group of lads, and it was like I was trying to run through treacle. Now there we were, in the field opposite the house, and Paul's dad kicked the ball so hard it came flying at me and smacked me on the left side of the head. My ears burned, my cheeks throbbed, and I wanted to just roll over and die, but I didn't want Paul's dad to feel bad, so I gritted my teeth and tried to laugh it off. His family howled – a day never goes by in their household when they don't laugh. It's the most beautiful melody in the universe.

There was a brief moment when I had to consider myself a dead man walking. Paul and I were housesitting for his parents while they were away. I was trawling through his mum's Sky TV guide and saw the memory was full, so deleted the entire collection of *Desperate Housewives* that was filling it up. I thought I was being helpful, doing her a favour. It turns out she'd spent years recording them to rewatch, and then I came along and obliterated the entire hard drive with the click of a button. Paul was furious; his mum wasn't too pleased, either. I took a *Desperate Housewives* DVD boxset round, and a sympathy card that had 'Sorry for the loss of your loving wife' printed on the front. She liked my dark sense of humour, appreciated the gesture, and we moved on. I didn't need to perform or calculate my every move with these people. They accepted me for all that I was.

★ ★ ★

One of the most powerful things about my partnership with Paul is that it seems to have changed my stepdad's views on homosexuality. At first, he found it difficult to digest and process – he admits that himself. But I think that is because he went to a boarding school where he witnessed terrible things happening to young lads. That kind of terror isn't something you can just forget, and I don't blame him one bit.

It's no surprise that Paul has turned out to be a good man, because he is descended from them. When I was depressed and sobbed furiously on his chest, he would hold me the way his mother holds her grandchildren – close and firm, protecting them from the world. He laughed like one sister and sometimes stropped like the other. I saw them as a perfectly imperfect family, and to share snippets of our lives together has been glorious.

These were just the rosy days of our new relationship, though, and we would both have to learn that love isn't always in bloom. But there is always hope, there's always the chance to share a life together, just like that great-uncle, who died recently with his partner of forty years – perhaps more – right by his side.

Pork Pies

———

MAKES 6

These certainly aren't the kind of pork pies Paul and I would share as we nestled down on a Saturday night in various hotels in Lancashire. The ones back then were the cheapest available from the shop, but they were delicious, nonetheless. This is a more elevated version – a recipe, in fact, that I used to teach my students at my cookery school. But I can't eat a pork pie now without thinking back to the early days of our relationship.

For the filling
150g (5½oz) pork shoulder, trimmed and very finely chopped
100g (3½oz) pork belly, trimmed and very finely chopped
6 rashers unsmoked streaky bacon, very finely chopped
1 small banana shallot, very finely chopped
3g fine salt
½ teaspoon mustard powder
½ teaspoon freshly grated nutmeg
½ teaspoon fine black pepper

For the hot water crust pastry
150g (5½oz) plain (all-purpose) flour, plus extra for dusting
150g (5½oz) strong white bread flour

5g (⅛oz) fine salt
125ml (4fl oz) water
110g (3¾oz) lard, cubed
1 egg yolk, beaten with a pinch of salt, to glaze

For the jelly
2 gelatine leaves
1 chicken stock pot/stock cube
200ml (7fl oz) apple juice

- Preheat the oven to 200°C/180°C fan/400°F/gas mark 6.

- Mix all the filling ingredients together in a bowl, ensuring everything is well combined, then set aside.

- For the pastry, tip the flours into a heatproof bowl. Put the salt, water and lard into a saucepan. Set the pan over a medium heat until the lard just about melts, then bring to the boil. Next, pour it into the bowl with the flours and beat vigorously with a wooden spoon until the mixture forms a rough dough. Tip the dough on to the counter (dusted with the smallest amount of flour) and knead briefly until smooth.

- Save a third of the dough for the lids, then roll out the rest on a lightly floured surface to a thickness of about 5mm (¼in). Cut out six discs, each big enough to line the base and sides of a muffin-tray cavity, with surplus hanging over the top – you may need to ball the dough back up and re-roll it. Fill the pastry cases with the meat mixture, pressing it down firmly and leaving a millimetre or so of space at the top.

- Roll out the remaining pastry, again on a lightly floured surface, and cut out six discs big enough to cover the pies, with a little surplus around the edge. Glaze the edges of the pastry cases with a little egg yolk. Cut a hole in the centre of each pastry lid, then pop them on top of the pies – I use the smaller tip of a piping nozzle for the hole. Press a fork firmly into the pastry all around the outer edge to seal the lid, then trim off any surplus and crimp all around. Glaze each pie with a little egg yolk before baking for 40 minutes, or until golden brown and a thermometer inserted into the centre reads at least 75°C (167°F). Remove from the oven.

- For the jelly, put the gelatine leaves in a bowl of cold water and leave them to soak and soften for 5 minutes. Put the cider and stock into a saucepan over a medium–high heat and once it reaches a simmer, remove it from the heat. Squeeze the excess water out of the gelatine leaves and add them to the stock. Transfer the stock to a jug, then carefully pour the stock into each pie through the hole in the lid – you'll need to add a little, let it settle, then top up. Allow the pies to cool to room temperature, then refrigerate overnight to set. These will keep for 3 days in the fridge.

Definitely Not His Mother's Corned Beef Hash

———

SERVES 2

Irene, Paul's mother, makes the most delicious corned beef hash, but she's never written the recipe down. She talked me through it, explaining how she uses a mixture of potatoes and even different types of corned beef, but I didn't want to even attempt to replicate it. It's sacred, almost. Hers is the wetter kind – more like a stew – whereas this recipe, which I make for special occasions like birthdays and Valentine's Day, is the dryer kind of hash. I like it with the crunch from a breadcrumb topping, and slightly caught in places – but it will never compare to Irene's.

400g (14oz) new potatoes, halved (or quartered if
they're on the large side)
30g (1oz) unsalted butter
1 carrot, coarsely grated
1 celery stick, coarsely grated
1 small onion, coarsely grated
340g can corned beef, chopped into 2cm (¾in) cubes
small handful of fresh parsley, roughly chopped
2 tablespoons Worcestershire sauce
40g (1½oz) breadcrumbs
2 eggs

415g (14½oz) can baked beans
brown sauce (or steak sauce), to serve

- Put the new potatoes into a pan, cover with water and bring to the boil over a high heat. Cook for 20–25 minutes or until tender and easily pierced with a knife, then drain.

- Preheat the oven to 200°C/180°C fan/400°F/gas mark 6.

- Melt the butter in an ovenproof frying pan over a medium–high heat, then add the carrot, celery and onion. Fry, stirring occasionally, for about 3 minutes, or until softened. Add the corned beef, parsley and Worcestershire sauce, along with the cooked, drained potatoes. Toss it all together, mash briefly with a potato masher to squash the potatoes, then scatter the breadcrumbs over the top. Transfer to the oven and bake for 20–25 minutes, or until slightly caught and crispy.

- When the hash is almost ready, fry the eggs to your liking and heat the beans according to the can instructions.

- Serve the hash with the beans on the side, and a fried egg each on top, with plenty of brown sauce (non-negotiable, as far as I'm concerned).

Meatballs

———

SERVES 4

Meatballs, in any form, have a special place on our table. Not only are they the first food I made after our long, joyful first date, but as our relationship progressed, Paul and I would regularly have little trips to Ikea. We'd imagine our future home and all its furniture, then dig into a plate of meatballs – though Swedish meatballs are very different from these.

For the meatballs
250g (9oz) minced (ground) pork
250g (9oz) minced (ground) beef
1 banana shallot, finely chopped
1 garlic clove, minced
2 teaspoons fennel seeds
3 tablespoons full-fat milk
1 large egg
25g (1oz) breadcrumbs
75g (2⅔oz) pecorino or Parmesan cheese, finely grated
small handful of flat-leaf parsley stalks, finely chopped

For the sauce
1 tablespoon olive oil

1 onion, finely sliced
1 garlic clove, minced
100ml (3½fl oz) white wine
400g (14oz) can chopped tomatoes
1 teaspoon balsamic vinegar
handful of flat-leaf parsley leaves, finely chopped
small handful of fresh basil, finely chopped

To serve
enough pasta of your choice for 4 people, cooked according
to packet instructions
freshly grated pecorino, to serve

- For the meatballs, mix all the ingredients in a large bowl, squishing everything together with your hands to combine. Divide into 24 small meatballs and set aside on a plate – to do this, I weigh the mixture, then divide the total weight by 24 and portion it out precisely. You can just eyeball it, if that's your preference.

- Preheat the oven to 240°C/220°C fan/475°F/gas mark 9.

- For the sauce, heat the oil in a medium ovenproof frying pan over a medium–high heat. Add the onion and fry, stirring occasionally, for 5–10 minutes, or until soft and translucent. Don't let it take on too much colour – you just need it to be softened and a little sweeter.

- Add the garlic and fry for a minute, then increase the heat to high and add the wine. Once the wine has almost fully reduced, add the tomatoes and vinegar. Bring to the boil, then reduce to a simmer and drop in the meatballs. I don't bother to brown my meatballs, because I want the fat to become part of the sauce, and I find there are already so many punchy flavours here that the flavour benefit of the Maillard reaction (the browning of meat) is only a little beneficial – but if you're the type who must brown their meatballs, do so before you fry the onions.

- Transfer the pan to the oven and bake for 10 minutes, then remove it to stir through the fresh herbs. Return to the oven for a further 5 minutes.

- Serve with pasta and pecorino cheese.

Sticky Toffee Pudding

―――――

SERVES 8–10

Paul's friend Sophie was one of the first people I met from Paul's life, and she was so caring and protective of us, her boys. She'd frequently make this sticky toffee pudding for us, and after a little persuasion, I managed to get the recipe off her. This is a tested and tweaked version, but I've been making it for over twelve years now, and I truly believe it's the best STP there is.

For the sponge
250g (9oz) dried pitted dates, chopped
1 teaspoon bicarbonate of soda (baking soda)
350g (12oz) boiling water
60g (2¼oz) unsalted butter, at room temperature, plus extra for greasing
250g (9oz) light brown muscovado sugar
2 large eggs
seeds from 1 vanilla pod
300g (10½oz) self-raising flour
½ teaspoon fine salt

For the sticky toffee sauce
225g (8oz) unsalted butter

300g (10½oz) dark brown muscovado sugar
200g (7oz) whipping cream

- An hour before you want to make the pudding, combine the dates, bicarb and hot water in a bowl and set aside to soak until the dates are mushy.

- Preheat the oven to 180°C/160°C fan/350°F/gas mark 4 and grease a 23 × 33cm (9 × 13in) roasting dish.

- Put the butter and sugar into a mixing bowl and beat with a handheld electric mixer until well combined – there's way more sugar than butter here, so this won't go fluffy. Add the eggs and vanilla, followed by the date mixture (including all the liquid), and beat until well combined. Sift over the flour and salt and fold in until you have a smooth, fairly loose batter.

- Pour the batter into the greased tray – it won't seem like there's enough, but there is – and bake for 30–40 minutes, or until the sponge is well risen and a skewer inserted into the centre comes out clean. Allow the sponge to cool slightly while you make the sauce.

- Put the ingredients for the sauce into a medium-sized saucepan and set over a medium heat. Stir until the butter melts and the sugar dissolves. Once you have a gorgeously glossy sauce, bring it to a boil for just a moment, then pour it over the baked, partially cooled sponge (still in the tray). At this stage, you can refrigerate or freeze the sticky toffee pudding, should you wish to do so.

- When you want to serve the pudding, preheat the oven to 180°C/160°C fan/350°F/gas mark 4 and bake it for 30 minutes, or until the sauce is bubbling and piping hot. Serve with lashings of cream, custard or ice cream – or do as I do, and go for all three.

4.

Scones in the Dock

———

Many people will have a similar story about their baking beginnings – cosied in the kitchen with some comforting maternal or paternal figure, licking cake batter from the beaters – and I am certainly no exception to this rule. Being together at work – the chippy or the dry-cleaner's – or tripping over one another in the kitchen, take up most of the memory space I have of time with Mum. Though one of the earliest and most vivid recollections I have is of her driving me to nursery school in a neighbouring village. I think at this point she had a pale-blue car, though it really doesn't matter. I remember looking at her in the bright sunlight of the late-spring mornings as she'd open her window just a crack and raise her nose to it while driving, telling me to smell the wild garlic. She was a beautiful woman. She still is. Her dark hair fluttered in the breeze from the window and her eyes shone emerald green in the low morning light. She looked happy, even though I hated going to that nursery school, and I undoubtedly made her life a misery on these mornings. I'd scream and thrash when she dropped me off. I didn't know at the time, but she would cry after she said goodbye and drove to work, often stopping at phone boxes to ring the nursery to make sure I was OK. I had this vision that the world would split into two while I was at nursery. Mum and my family would be on one side and I'd be stuck, alone, on the other as it hurtled through the universe. I hated it there, not least because the owner used to pretend she had naughty children shackled in the loft. We'd have to throw torn pieces of old carpet through the hatch for them to eat. I guess it was a scare tactic to maintain order, but come on – that's a pretty intense tale to tell a gullible gaggle of three-year-olds.

I don't think we ever ate wild garlic at home. We certainly never foraged it. In fact, I'm not sure I tried it until much later in life, after I'd won *Bake Off* and had moved to Greenwich in London. My dad came to visit one weekend to help me put up some wallpaper. We walked around Oxleas Wood and picked carrier bags full of the stuff. Back at my apartment, I washed it and made flatbreads with anchovies, olives and wild garlic butter.

Baking with Mum was always a great comfort. She wasn't, and still isn't, a particularly artistic baker. Whenever she makes a pavlova, she puts so much sparkle on it – edible glitter and chocolate stars – it looks like a drag queen exploded all over it. But everything is always perfect in its imperfection. I remember the way she'd make butterfly cakes. She'd insert the knife into the top of each cooled cake and remove a little cone of sponge – rather like how I was *supposed* to remove eyes from potatoes when I came to be a potato-peeler. Then, together, we'd spoon whipped cream into the cavities. Looking back, the cream was overwhipped – on the verge of turning to butter, mealy in its texture as opposed to smooth and voluptuous – but it didn't matter a jot. Once we'd dolloped on a little blob of jam, the reserved cone of sponge would be split down the middle and placed on top of the cake to resemble butterfly wings. Finished with a snowfall of icing sugar, they were just perfect.

At least, I *think* I remember standing beside her on a chair, helping throughout the process, but that memory could quite easily be fiction. We often weave extra fibres into the fabric of our recollection, and that may be the case here. But the feeling is undeniable: loving safety.

Perhaps that's why food is such a comfort to many of us; it forms a huge part of our identity. Whether that's a larger-scale cultural or geographical identity, or something a little smaller and more personal, what and how we eat is inextricably linked to who we are. Whenever I eat a box of chocolates now, I'm once again sitting on the couch with Mum, Dad and my sisters, watching *Casualty*. And yet even that memory comes with complications: after a while, Dad realised I'd been guzzling the chocolates more quickly than everyone else. He told me off for being greedy, and from then on, I was only allowed to take a chocolate whenever he said so; once the rest of the family had taken two, I was allowed one.

My parents seemed to have very different attitudes towards food, and that is perfectly illustrated by porridge. I can still see

Dad making his porridge in the morning with an egg cup. He'd have precisely the same amount each day – never too much – and would finish it with a just little sugar or syrup. He was repetitive and restrained, much like I've had to be in recent years to prevent myself from having a bulimic binge and purge. Mum, on the other hand, is nothing short of decadent when it comes to her oats. I once caught her bent down at the freezer, scooping ice cream into her bowl. What a legend.

I suppose it has something to do with the fact my father was born in the early 1940s, just as the Second World War was winding up. The socio-economic mindset would still, perhaps, have been very much based on rationing and restraint, and I wonder if that influenced Dad's perspective of 'I don't live to eat, I eat to live!'. For my mother, an early-60s baby, I think it's safe to say the opposite is true. As a result, I fall somewhere in the middle. I love and celebrate food, but I am afraid of what it can do. I'm not scared, necessarily, of getting fat – though that is, of course, a concern for many people with a body dysmorphic disorder – but of my potential to simply never stop eating. And I don't say that flippantly or humorously; it is a fear that rears its head regularly.

Dad did (and still does) love a treat, though. Pick 'n' mix was always something we'd get together. Every Saturday, we'd cross the road to Brian's shop – a little newsagent's in the village where I grew up – and get a quarter (of a pound) of mix, and I'd be so excited to untwist the top of the paper bag and dig in.

I think his restraint stemmed from his Catholic upbringing,

too. His father, who was in the merchant navy, was absent for most of his youth, so his mother had to tie them down with the ligature of religion, just to muddle through. Dad definitely was never one to follow rules, but he still seemed to long for something – a sense of structure and belonging perhaps. Or maybe an escape from who he really was? When decorating his new house after he moved out, he somehow got involved with the Mormon church – they came knocking, offered to help strip the wallpaper, and seduced Dad into their community. For a while, Our Vic and I would accompany him to temple on a Sunday. We even switched from coffee to *Caro* to renounce caffeine. We really joined the gang. Dad and Our Vic were baptised, but Mum wouldn't let me be – I was far too young, eight or nine, perhaps. I think eventually she put a stop to us going. I was glad; I'd had enough of bloated old men in suits wanting to shake my hand. I had a wart on my right forefinger, so would try to shake hands with the elders with that finger folded down. They always looked at me like I was odd.

* * *

After baking with Mum at an early age – probably four or five years old – I don't think I did it again until much later, when I was at high school. In home economics one afternoon, we learned how to make microwaveable cakes in those red plastic domes left over from Christmas puddings. I became obsessed with them, and Mum would often come home from a shift at the chip shop to find I'd made microwave cakes of many colours – mostly green. I'd root through the cupboards in search of baking ingredients, and we always had those little bottles – I can't remember whether plastic or glass – of liquid food colouring, where the metal screw top tended to be so covered in the colouring that when you went to open it, your fingertips became stained for days. I still recall the strong, sweet, eggy scent that would fill the kitchen as the microwave's turntable rotated and the cake rapidly cooked.

Aside from those colourfully experimental efforts, baking was a forgotten hobby until after I dropped out of Oxford and got that full-time job in a call centre dealing with car insurance. At some point along the way, I had to take a few days off because my depression was so bad. But, as is usually the case, it was concomitant with mania, and one day I found myself baking quite frantically. I don't remember the process, but I can still see the rhubarb pie, the angel food cake and the hummingbird cake lined up on the kitchen table, slightly caught and burned from the harsh heat of mum's Aga. It was clear from that day that baking would become a great source of comfort for me. The homeliness of it gave me a sense of identity – naturally connecting me to my mum – but the power of its artistry allowed me to experiment, which at that time was a direct reflection of where I was as a person: I was making that huge and fundamental transition from boy to man.

That transition period isn't a simple move from A to B. It's a purgatory, where the excuse of youthful misjudgement slowly metamorphoses into expectation of responsibility for choices and actions. I felt that after dropping out of Oxford; those who expected me to go – my mum and stepdad – saw my leaving as a reckless disregard for a certain and comfortable future.

Their disappointment was something I had to deal with, but I was shielded by my sense of self. I *knew* I didn't want to study *that* course at *that* institution, in spite (or perhaps even *because*) of the air of privilege that existed around it, and I'm deeply proud of that self-possession. And besides, it's not like I sat at home doing nothing; I put myself out there and found a job.

★ ★ ★

The car insurance job was only ever a stopgap; though I can't deny the value of chatting to a customer on the phone while working on the computer. That was a skill set that would serve me well when I came to work in television and have detailed debates on the sofa with a noisy gallery chatting in my ear. Never underestimate the importance or opportunity of a job, big or small. When I started a new degree course – law – at the University of Manchester, I'd spend the summer and Christmas breaks working in the local tearoom back home. The girls who ran it encouraged me to make a few bits for the counter. The first time I made a hummingbird cake for the café, I hadn't quite got the shelves in the oven level, so the cakes came out wonky. I didn't know at that time how to trim cakes to make them level, nor had I learned that buttercream could mask a multitude of sins, so the finished cake was more slanted than the one Fauna made for Aurora's sixteenth birthday in Disney's *Sleeping Beauty*. Not wanting to scaffold it in place with a broom like the gentle fairy, I drove wooden kebab skewers deep into the layers to hold the whole thing together. Thankfully, I was on the coffee counter, so if anyone asked for a slice, I'd quickly and discreetly fling the kebab skewers over my shoulder to hide my questionable construction method.

As with most things in life, practice makes perfect, and the more I baked, experimented and, most importantly, learned from my many mistakes, the better I became. It helped that I moved into a student flat with an electric oven – I'm sorry Aga-lovers, Mary Berry included, but I don't think I could ever trust myself or the Aga to get anything baking-related just right.

The more stressful my law course became, the more I'd find myself seeking refuge in that little kitchen, making focaccia and fougasse, Swiss rolls and macarons. So obsessed was I with mastering the art of macarons, I went through bag after bag of ground almonds. Most of my university companions were spending their spare cash on vodka and condoms; luckily, I had Paul to supply both of those, so my limited funds could be directed towards my new obsession. I didn't have a car, so I'd walk to the biggest supermarket, about three miles away, to get my utensils and ingredients. More often than not, though, I'd return to find I'd forgotten something, and would have to trundle back.

As food became more of a comfort than ever, it also became something of an emotional terrorist. If I ate more than my calorie tracker allowed – which, looking back, was a worryingly low 1,200 calories a day – I would make myself go to the gym twice in one day to balance it out. I never really liked cardio, but I'd force myself to do it vigorously if I had overindulged. That's the problem when exercise isn't undertaken for pleasure – it can quickly become an evil, twisted form of torture, and striking the balance is so incredibly difficult.

When I started college, I was undoubtedly anorexic. I'd gone from being a fairly solid lad in the last year of high school, to a tall, thin streak of piss. My tutors at college were concerned; they'd bring it up with me or Mum at parents' evening, but we all just brushed it off as a growth spurt or hormones. The truth is, I wasn't eating. I'd have soup for lunch and an evening meal, which for a six-foot-two lad just wasn't enough. I'd spend my evenings in my bedroom lifting weights without any real plan or routine, before drinking glasses of creatine dissolved in water. I got thin and gaunt. Some people would call me 'the model' as they pouted and stuck out their cheekbones when we passed each other in the corridor.

I did end up doing a little modelling towards the end of college, after coming second in *The Face of Wigan* competition (as unglamorous as it sounds). Groups of well-arranged lads and lasses had to choose an outfit from Debenhams then parade it down a catwalk in front of the judging panel, made up of a journalist from a local newspaper and agents from a Manchester modelling agency. Although I did not win, the agents signed me up anyway. I'd already changed my name at the start of college, taking my grandfather's surname to make it more showbiz. My birth name, John Cunningham, was too clumsy for anyone who was going to make it in the arts. But I think dispensing with my dad's surname really upset him.

My poor mum had to drive me from test shoot to test shoot,

where I'd insist she waited in the car for hours, while I posed for the cameras. I didn't like her watching me; I felt like she'd judge me or tell me how to hold myself – she was always forcibly trying to rearrange my shoulders as I slouched in a chair.

After a while, I got my first paid gig – for a school uniform catalogue. My visions of being sat in underpants in a sailboat on the Italian Riviera like David Gandy were dashed, as I sweated under a nylon jumper, choked by a tie. I was destined, I'm afraid, to sport a raincoat, plonked in a dinghy somewhere on the Norfolk Broads. Eventually I put a little weight on, and the agency pointed that out saying, 'You were a waif when we signed you'. I decided to leave.

I'd dabbled in making myself sick back in college. I'd chat with a lad I fancied on MSN messenger, and his constant rejection made me want to stuff myself with buttered toast – sometimes as many as ten slices – even after my dinner. Feeling guilty for the binge, I'd then force it out of me, but that had only happened a handful of times. Now, though, in my Manchester apartment, playing the role of the independent law student who had his life on track, I was slowly falling apart. Binges and purges became more frequent, but none of us – Paul, my flatmate Holly or me – would ever feel it was a concern. It was just John being greedy again, followed by the guilt. We ignored it, but it didn't ignore me. It *had* me. Eating disorders thrive under the veil of secrecy and shame. Mine didn't have just a veil, it lurked behind an invisibility cloak.

Even now, as I sit having just eaten a bowl of haggis potato hash, in a cabin in Scotland, writing this book, not a day goes by when I don't worry about what or how much I eat. It is haunting. It is exhausting. It takes over my life and I feel helpless. I just wish I could enjoy my food without the pangs of hunger being replaced by even louder pangs of guilt.

I'm working on it.

★ ★ ★

Whenever I went home in the holidays and purged, Mum would find little pieces of evidence, like a drip down the front of the toilet. She'd ask me if I was making myself sick, but I denied it. I was ashamed of what she'd think of me. I already felt like such a disappointment: gay, Oxford dropout, useless at sport. If I'd told her back then, I don't think she'd have understood. We were quite a 'stiff upper lip' family. We didn't wallow in our misery; we just pulled our socks up and got on with whatever life threw at us. I don't hold that against any of my family, because we've all changed. We've all softened and become more empathetic and kinder. But I do wonder, if we'd been the softer permutation of ourselves back then, would I still be struggling to keep my food down now?

What's interesting, though, is that beyond the secrecy of my bulimia, I started to blossom as a man. My law course made me more confident and feistier. Don't get me wrong, I'd never *not* been confident – I'd performed on stage since the age of three or four and was part of my local drama and dance group throughout my teenage years – but for the first time, I felt a sense of pride in myself beyond the resounding applause of an audience. I liked who I was becoming and my sense of morality. I'd happily debate with lecturers in front of an auditorium of my peers about jurisprudence or criminal evidence, and not for the attention, but because I believed strongly in my arguments – arguments into which I'd put nights of research and reading.

On one particular law-firm vacation scheme (which basically involved doing work experience for a firm during the Easter or summer holidays), we were asked to create a presentation on something about which we were passionate. Someone talked about Dante, someone waxed lyrical about Charles Saatchi, and I'm sure another person rambled on about Paul Rand, the American art director. I arrived with a huge Tupperware tub absolutely rammed to the brim with scones. I must have made fifty or sixty. I plonked them on the table – there were, at most, fifteen of us in the room – along with a jar of jam and a tub of clotted cream, and mumbled on about scones: the origin, the name, the correct pronunciation. I think people thought I was mad. Perhaps I was. I was certainly obsessed.

I spent years trying to perfect a scone recipe. They came out too dry, too crumbly, too cakey, too soft. Looking back, the ones I made for that presentation were terrible: the kind that needed thick layers of butter, jam and cream (not necessarily in that order; I don't want to offend anyone in either Devon or Cornwall!) to even be swallowable. I only managed to perfect my recipes because Rosemary Shrager's patisserie chef, Mark, gave me a clue one day when we were filming a series for ITV. I begged him for the recipe, but he simply shook his head, then held up his finger and said, in his strong French accent, 'I'll give you a single clue – crème fraîche!'

That was the code I'd needed to crack – the ingredients. I dabbled with different quantities of both buttermilk and crème fraîche. I experimented with kneading and resting, and after a dozen or so attempts, I'd mastered what I now consider to be the perfect scone. It's the recipe of which I am most proud, and I'm so grateful to Mark for the life-changing tip. Serendipity at its finest.

★ ★ ★

It was during university that I started a food blog – *Flour and Eggs* – where I'd share recipes and ramble on about food and how much I loved it. After his death, I learned that my grandfather, Merrick, had never missed a post, and read them proudly on his iPad. His last words to Mum, as she accompanied him in the ambulance and he faded out of consciousness for a final time, were, 'I have to live to see John win *Bake Off*.'

He'd longed to see me graduate Oxford, but obviously never did. Nor did he live to see me win *Bake Off* on television, though I'm glad I told him the day I won – he suffered a brain aneurism shortly afterwards and never woke up. We sat beside his bed as we turned off his life support, but in death – as in life – he fought. It took him a couple of weeks to die. We had the opportunity to say our goodbyes, which we whispered gently into his ear. Never in life had I told him that I loved him, but I made sure to say it as he lay on that hospital bed, surrounded by his family.

I'll never forget his last words to me, on the phone as I returned triumphant from the *Bake Off* tent: 'What a guy!'

It was actually my grandfather who responded the most positively when I came out as gay. When my mum told him, naturally prepared for the flak one might expect from a man born in the 1930s, he replied, 'Well, we won't love him any less, will we?' He simply didn't have a problem with it, and when I brought my first boyfriend from college home, my grandfather engaged with him in conversation and treated him as a human. I like to think that his years on the farm, caring for his flock of sheep, taught him that love, in its basic form, is quite simply to be kind. There were never eggshells to dance upon with my grandfather. I wish I'd got to know him more. I feel many of the positive things with which I identify myself come from him: my love of animals; my longing to be out in the wild; my work ethic and focus (though that certainly came to me from both of my parents, too).

★ ★ ★

My food blog became even more colourful and experimental as I watched the first two series of *The Great British Bake Off*. Paul, Holly and I would cosily convene on our couches – of which we had many in the flat, because if I wasn't spending my money on ground almonds and other baking ingredients, I spent it on couches from charity shops to try and make our flat as homely as possible; in retrospect, it resembled a community centre more than a student apartment. But I think I did this because, for the first time since leaving the first house I grew up in, I felt safe. For the first time in many years, I didn't fear the dark or sleeping alone.

There we were, a little non-nuclear family, enjoying a TV show together that would eventually go on to change my life. Every week I'd try to mimic what the on-screen bakers had had to make in the 'technical challenge' – the round where the recipe is pared back and a complete surprise. We'd whizz to Sainsbury's before the credits had even rolled and buy the ingredients to make whatever they'd created on the show. It became more than a distraction from my law degree, more than a hobby; it became an utter obsession. I'd look beyond the baking books to food scientists – specifically Harold McGee – for reasons why reactions happened the way they did in baking. I'd get lost in that side of it, and found hours could pass by as I flicked through the pages.

For a friend's birthday I made a croquembouche – a towering cone of profiteroles filled with crème pâtissière, glued in their pinpoint formation by caramel. I'd spent my last few quid for the week on gold leaf – which, like a magpie, I became obsessed with – and delicately placed it on the amber caramel structure. I stood back and realised I had a talent for this. A natural creative talent? Yes. But my obsessive nature also meant that I'd spent hours honing these technical and scientific skills. It was in that moment, as I stood before a Parisian masterpiece in a terraced house in Bolton, that I knew I could make this into a career.

Shortly afterwards, I sent an application form to Love Productions for the third series of *The Great British Bake Off*. At the front of my application form was a picture of me finessing that croquembouche. Within days, the phone rang. The production company had received my application, and wanted to know more.

Butterfly Cakes

———

MAKES 8

Mum's butterfly cakes are undoubtedly my earliest memory of cake. They were so rustic – the tops were probably lobbed off unevenly, and the cream was certainly overwhipped and slightly mealy – but the rules of baking perfection upon which I try to build my recipes these days didn't exist to me back then. These were the edible embodiment of motherly love.

For the cakes
115g (4oz) Stork baking spread (or margarine)
115g (4oz) caster (superfine) sugar
115g (4oz) self-raising flour
¼ teaspoon fine salt
2 large eggs

For the filling
150ml (5fl oz) double (heavy) cream
2 tablespoons icing (confectioners') sugar, plus extra to dust
1 tablespoon vanilla bean paste
8 teaspoons jam (I like blackcurrant)

- Preheat the oven to 180°C/160°C fan/350°F/gas mark 4. Line 8 holes of a 12-hole muffin tin with paper muffin cases.

- In a mixing bowl, beat the baking spread, sugar, flour and salt into a thick paste – I use a handheld electric beater, as Mum did, but you could do this in a stand mixer, too. Add the eggs and beat just until you have a smooth batter, then divide evenly between the muffin cases. Bake for 12–15 minutes, or until a skewer inserted into the centre comes out completely clean, then leave to cool completely on a wire rack.

- To prepare the filling, whip the cream with the icing sugar and vanilla, just until it holds its shape but still threatens to sink back into itself.

- Using a small, sharp knife, cut a shallow cone out of the top of each cooled cake. Fill that hole with a teaspoon of jam, then top with a liberal blob of whipped cream. Cut the cone of cake in half and arrange the two pieces, like butterfly wings, on top of the cream. Dust with icing sugar and serve. These will keep for a day or two in an airtight container.

Scone mania

If I've had one unhealthy obsession in life, I think scones would
be it. I'm not kidding. There were days in the past, when,
in pursuit of the perfect scone, I would bake as many as ten
different batches to try and get my recipe just right. It should
therefore come as no surprise that when I finally did nail down
the perfect recipe – thanks to that French pastry chef, Mark – I
tested many different versions. These are my favourites.

———

Perfect Plain Scones

MAKES 10–12

These are the scones we make in the afternoon tea class at my cookery school, and they are the lightest, fluffiest beauties I've ever had. There's no real trickery to making them, just a process that most domestic scone recipes omit: resting the dough. This not only allows any gluten to relax and soften, but also enables the baking powder to react, filling the dough with plenty of air. An important part is the working of the dough. It must be kneaded just until smooth – overdo it, and you risk the dough being tough and dense.

150ml (5fl oz) buttermilk
150g (5½oz) full-fat crème fraîche
1 teaspoon lemon juice
450g (1lb) plain (all-purpose) flour, plus extra for dusting
15g (½oz) baking powder
80g (2¾oz) caster (superfine) sugar
pinch of fine sea salt
80g (2¾oz) unsalted butter, cubed, plus extra for greasing
1 large egg yolk, beaten with a pinch of salt

- Put the buttermilk, crème fraîche and lemon juice into a jug and mix together. The mixture is supposed to curdle, so don't throw it out.

- In a mixing bowl, combine the flour, baking powder, caster sugar and salt. Add the butter and rub together with your fingers until the butter is evenly dispersed through the dry ingredients and the mixture resembles breadcrumbs. Pour the wet ingredients into the bowl and start to mix – either with your hand or a wooden spoon – until the mixture comes together into a scraggy mass.

- Tip the dough on to a lightly floured worktop and knead very briefly – for no more than a minute or so – until it is smooth. It should be firm enough to hold its shape, but still tender and yielding to a poke. Put the dough on to a greased tray and cover with clingfilm (plastic wrap). Leave to rest for 30 minutes.

- Flour the worktop lightly and tip the rested dough on to it. Pat the dough down with a floured hand until about 2cm (¾in) thick. Cut out your scones using a 6cm (2½in) cookie cutter. Set them on a greased tray, cover with clingfilm again and leave to rest for a further 15 minutes.

- Preheat the oven to 200°C/180°C fan/400°F/gas mark 6.

- Once the scones have rested, flip them over so their flat bottoms become perfectly flat tops. If you position the scones fairly close together, with just enough room in between to allow for swelling, they will steam as they bake and stay softer. Glaze the tops of the scones with the egg yolk, then bake for 12–15 minutes, or until the tops are deeply golden and the bases are just gently browned. The scones will still feel very soft, but they will firm up a little as they cool. Slide them on to a cooling rack and allow them to cool just enough so that you can slather one liberally with cream and jam and eat it without burning your mouth. These are best eaten fresh, but can be stored in an airtight tin for a couple of days.

Blueberry and Lemon Glazed Scones

———

MAKES 8

These are a variation of my original scone recipe, but rather than just adding it as a variation, it's easier to explain it from start to finish, with all the ingredients in the right order. These are cut and baked in fat triangular wedges, much like the American-style scones you get in coffee houses in the US. The added beauty here lies in the extra hit of sweetness from the bright-purple glaze. I'd serve these with clotted cream and a sharp blackcurrant jam. You'll notice that I don't rest these as I do the scones on page 129, and that's simply because the plain scones need to be impossibly light. I prefer these ones ever so slightly denser and cakier.

150ml (5fl oz) buttermilk
150g (5½oz) full-fat crème fraîche
zest of 1 lemon and 1 teaspoon lemon juice
450g (1lb) plain (all-purpose) flour, plus extra for dusting
15g (½oz) baking powder
80g (2¾oz) caster (superfine) sugar
pinch of fine sea salt
80g (2¾oz) unsalted butter, cubed, plus extra for greasing
100g (3½oz) frozen blueberries
1 large egg yolk, beaten with a pinch of salt

For the glaze
40g (1½oz) frozen blueberries, defrosted
40g (1½oz) full-fat milk
25g (1oz) unsalted butter
250g (9oz) icing (confectioners') sugar

- Preheat the oven to 200°C/180°C fan/400°F/gas mark 6.

- Put the buttermilk, crème fraîche and lemon juice into a jug and mix together. The mixture is supposed to curdle, so don't throw it out.

- In a mixing bowl, combine the flour with the baking powder, caster sugar, lemon zest and salt. Add the butter and rub together with your fingers until the butter is evenly dispersed through the dry ingredients and the mixture resembles breadcrumbs. Add the blueberries and toss through, then add the wet ingredients and start to mix – either with your hand or a wooden spoon – until the mixture comes together into a scraggy mass.

- Tip the dough on to a lightly floured worktop and knead very briefly – for no more than a minute or so – until it is smooth. It should be firm enough to hold its shape, but still tender and yielding to a poke.

- Flatten the dough into a thick disc (about 3cm/1¼in thick) and cut into eight wedges. Arrange these, well spaced out, on a baking sheet. Glaze with the beaten egg and bake for 12–15 minutes, or until puffed up and golden.

- Meanwhile, make the glaze. Combine the blueberries, milk and butter in a small saucepan over a high heat and bring to a boil, then remove from the heat and pour into a mixing bowl with the icing sugar. Whisk vigorously, breaking down some of the blueberries (ideally, you would use an immersion blender to blend until very smooth – but don't buy one just for this).

- Dunk the tops of the scones into the glaze. Let the glaze set, then dunk and leave to set again before serving. These are best served fresh, but will last for a couple of days stored in an airtight container.

Pumpkin Spice Scones

———

MAKES 8

This is my second-favourite variation of my perfect scone recipe, using the classic autumn combination of spice and pumpkin. I get the pumpkin from a can – which I buy online – but if you wanted to, you could steam your own. And if the season isn't right for pumpkin, sweet potato purée would also work.

150ml (5fl oz) buttermilk
150g (5½oz) canned pumpkin purée
1 teaspoon lemon juice
450g (1lb) plain (all-purpose) flour, plus extra for dusting
15g (½oz) baking powder
80g (2¾oz) caster (superfine) sugar
1 teaspoon ground cinnamon
½ teaspoon ground ginger
¼ teaspoon ground cardamom
¼ teaspoon ground allspice
⅛ teaspoon ground cloves
¼ teaspoon ground nutmeg
pinch of fine sea salt
80g (2¾oz) unsalted butter, cubed, plus extra
for greasing

1 large egg yolk, beaten with a pinch of salt
small handful of pumpkin seeds (optional)
small handful of pearl sugar (optional)

- Preheat the oven to 200°C/180°C fan/400°F/gas mark 6.

- Put the buttermilk, pumpkin purée and lemon juice into a jug and mix together. The mixture is supposed to curdle, so don't throw it out.

- In a mixing bowl, combine the flour with the baking powder, caster sugar, spices and salt. Add the butter and rub together with your fingers until the butter is evenly dispersed through the dry ingredients and the mixture resembles breadcrumbs. Add the wet ingredients and start to mix – either with your hand or a wooden spoon – until the mixture comes together into a scraggy mass.

- Tip the dough on to a lightly floured worktop and knead very briefly – for no more than a minute or so – until it is smooth. It should be firm enough to hold its shape, but still tender and yielding to a poke.

- Flour the worktop lightly and tip the dough on to it. Pat the dough down, with a floured hand, until about 3cm (1¼in) thick. Cut into eight wedges and arrange on a baking sheet, spaced well apart. Glaze the tops with the beaten egg and sprinkle on some pumpkin seeds and pearl sugar, if using. Bake for 12–15 minutes, or until golden and puffed up. Serve slightly warm. These will last a couple of days if stored in an airtight container.

Funfetti Birthday Cake Scones

————

MAKES 10–12

I don't need to write a whole new recipe here, because a few minor tweaks to my original recipe (page 129) will give you the sweetest little scones, spiked heavily with vanilla and filled with multicoloured funfetti sprinkles for extra flavour and crunch.

To the crème fraîche and buttermilk, add 2 tablespoons vanilla bean paste, and to the dry ingredients, add 60g (2¼oz) funfetti rainbow sprinkles.

Once they're baked, you can dunk the scones into a glaze made by beating together 40ml (1½fl oz) warmed full-fat milk, 25g (1oz) melted unsalted butter, 50g (1¾oz) full-fat cream cheese and 250g (9oz) icing (confectioners') sugar. Double-dunk the cooled scones into the glaze, then finish with an extra sprinkling of sprinkles. These will last a couple of days if stored in an airtight container.

Microwave Mug Cake

MAKES 1

I didn't know whether I should include this recipe – it seems a little bit silly in some ways. But then I had a harsh word with myself. This is a book of my truth, and microwave cakes were such an important part of my teenage years. They gave me a little project at the end of a school day, and they probably rekindled my love of baking. They're also something I make quite a bit if I want a little sweet treat after my tea, but don't want to make a full cake. I'm unashamed of this mug of delicious silliness.

1 tablespoon cocoa powder
2 tablespoons caster (superfine) sugar
2 tablespoons plain (all-purpose) flour
⅛ teaspoon baking powder
1 egg yolk
2 tablespoons sunflower oil
2 tablespoons full-fat milk
20g (¾oz) chocolate chips

• Simply throw all the ingredients into a mug and mix until smooth – though, of course, it will be studded with chocolate chips. Microwave on high for 45–90 seconds (mine takes 60), or until cooked through. Eat with lashings of double cream.

Wild Garlic, Anchovy and Olive Flatbreads

———

MAKES 4

I can't pass a sea of wild garlic without thinking back fondly to those journeys to nursery with Mum, when she'd wind down the car windows and tell me to smell the garlic as we drove through the dappled morning light. This recipe came about much later, when my dad and I took a walk through the woodland, foraging for wild garlic, near the first flat Paul and I ever bought.

200g (7oz) self-raising flour, plus extra for dusting
1 teaspoon fine salt
130ml (4½fl oz) lager
4 anchovies from a jar, roughly chopped
8 pitted green olives, roughly chopped
about 6 wild garlic leaves, roughly chopped,
plus a couple of flowers for decoration
6 tablespoons olive or rapeseed oil
sea salt flakes and coarse black pepper

• To make the bread, simply mix the flour with the salt and lager in a large bowl. Bring together into a rough dough, then knead on the worktop for a few minutes, or until smooth. Return the dough to the bowl, cover with clingfilm (plastic wrap) and leave to rest for 15 minutes.

- For the topping, combine the anchovies, olives and wild garlic leaves in a saucepan with the oil. Set over a high heat, just until the oil gets hot, then remove from the heat and leave the flavours to infuse into the oil.

- Divide the rested dough equally into four. On a lightly floured worktop, roll out each portion of dough to a circle about 20cm (8in) in diameter.

- Heat a frying pan over a high heat and, once hot, add the flatbreads, one at a time. Fry for a minute, or until the topside becomes slightly bumpy, then flip it over and fry the other side for a minute or so more. You don't want it to burn, but there's nothing wrong with a few bits of char. If you're cooking on gas, remove the flatbread from the pan – with kitchen tongs – and hold it directly over the flame for 10 seconds. It should swell up slightly. Remove from the heat and set aside on a plate while you cook the rest.

- Top each flatbread with the infused oil – bits and all – and serve with the garlic flowers scattered over. Finish with a sprinkling of sea salt and black pepper.

Hummingbird Bundt Cake

———

SERVES 10–12

I made this cake for my birthday during lockdown. It was hot and humid, and I couldn't face stacking a cake up with cream cheese frosting in that heat – it would have surely ended up wonky and leaning, like the hummingbird cake I made for the café counter back in the summer holidays while at university.

For the bundt tin lining paste
2 tablespoons vegetable shortening
2 tablespoons plain (all-purpose) flour
2 tablespoons sunflower oil

For the cake
100g (3½oz) pecans
340g (12oz) self-raising flour
340g (12oz) caster (superfine) sugar
1 teaspoon fine salt
2 teaspoons ground cinnamon
1 teaspoon ground ginger
½ teaspoon ground nutmeg
¼ teaspoon ground cloves
340g (12oz) ripe bananas

200g (7oz) pineapple chunks from a can (drained weight)
60ml (4 tablespoons) dark rum (or milk)
3 large eggs
180ml (6fl oz) sunflower oil

For the glaze
250g (9oz) icing (confectioners') sugar
40ml (1½fl oz) full-fat milk, warmed
1 tablespoon vanilla bean paste
30g (1oz) unsalted butter, melted
50g (1¾oz) full-fat cream cheese

- For the lining paste, simply beat together the vegetable shortening and flour in a bowl with a handheld electric mixer until well combined, then beat in the oil until you have a thick, white paste. Paint this liberally into a 10-cup capacity bundt tin (that's about 2.5 litres, but bundt tins tend to be measured in cup sizes, so I'm sticking to that here!), ensuring you get it in all the nooks and crannies.

- Preheat the oven to 200°C/180°C fan/400°F/gas mark 6. Scatter the pecans on to a roasting tray and roast for 5–10 minutes, or until they smell strongly but are only just starting to brown. Allow them to cool, then roughly chop and set aside.

- Reduce the oven temperature to 170°C/150°C fan/340°F/gas mark 3½.

- To make the cake, whisk together the flour, sugar, salt and spices in a large mixing bowl.

- In a second bowl, mash the bananas into a thick paste, then crush the pineapple chunks and add those to the paste as well. Beat in the rum, eggs and oil, then pour this mixture into the dry ingredients and fold together. Once you have a smooth batter, punctuated by chunks of banana and pineapple, fold in the roasted pecans, then pour the mixture into the prepared bundt tin and bake for 60–80 minutes (mine took precisely 75 minutes). When it's ready, a skewer inserted into the cake should come out fairly clean, with perhaps a few smears of pineapple or banana. Allow the cake to cool in the tin for 5 minutes, then invert on to a wire rack set over a plate or tray (to catch drips later) and allow to cool completely.

- For the glaze, sift the icing sugar into a large bowl. Add the warm milk, vanilla bean paste, melted butter and cream cheese and whisk until smooth and thick. Pour the glaze liberally over the cooled cake. Slice to serve. This will keep for about 4 days in an airtight container.

5.

The Big White Circus Tent

I had my first meeting with the producers of *The Great British Bake Off* on Halloween 2011. I'd recently started my third and final year of law school, so Mum was naturally worried it would derail me at the last hurdle. I knew it would be a lot to balance the finals of a law degree with filming a huge TV talent show, but I believed I could do it. I'd had enough of submitting, rolling over in fear and feeling like a puppet. I was determined to do what *I* wanted to do, to make myself proud.

As I always did for whatever event I was going to, I arrived in London a few hours early, eager as hell. My sister Victoria would often ask me 'Did you wet the bed?', as I turned up early for everything. Ever since arriving late and embarrassed for a primary school nativity play in church, I've always vowed to be early. I trundled down Woburn Place with my bakes in a tote bag. I felt nervous – of course I did – but mostly excited. I knew I had a talent for baking, and something inside me knew that I was going to get on the show – though I never, not in a million years, thought I would win it. It wasn't a grandiose cockiness; it was a calm sense of acknowledgement of the hours I had put into my hobby, my passion.

We'd been instructed to bring two bakes, one savoury and one sweet, which I'd been up all night baking, trying to get precisely right. I took my Rich Bitch Macarons – a chocolate shell filled with a champagne buttercream and strawberry jam, finished with gold leaf – and my Stuffed Piggy Pork Pies – filled with pork shoulder, pork loin, an apricot and thyme stuffing and a cider jelly. I sat with the food producer and home economist at a table in the middle of a room. In every corner was another person – producers, I assume. The food producer giggled when I told her the name I'd given to the macarons. 'I'm sure Mary Berry would love that,' she said. I couldn't tell whether she was being serious or sarcastic, but I laughed anyway.

After that brief meeting, I sat in front of a camera lit by a few filming lights and chatted to a producer about my life. It was the same lovely producer who'd called me a few weeks before. She asked me about my personal life, whether I had a partner. I told her I had a boyfriend, but that I didn't want to talk too much about that. I played it down and said it wasn't a serious relationship. I threw myself and the love of my life under a bus because that's what I thought they wanted to hear. I did worry they might not want me if I were overly camp, and I was concerned the audience wouldn't be able to look past it and appreciate me for my baking skills. I was once more that boy in the chip shop, serving burly blokes their chips and gravy.

Within a few weeks, I was back down in London, this time meeting Mary and Paul – the judges. I had to bake a batch of scones, according to Paul's recipe; again, I stayed up all night, trying to perfect them. I was plonked in front of the judges, who stood on the other side of a table. I was taken aback by how blue both pairs of eyes were. I glanced at Paul enquiringly, desperately trying to figure out whether he was wearing bright-blue contact lenses. Surely no one's eyes could be *so* blue. Elizabeth Taylor's, perhaps, but hers were a darker blue, almost purple. These were glacial.

Mary tore one of my scones in half and prodded it with her fingernail the way an inquisitive child might prod a dead bird with a twig. They didn't eat any of it, I don't think; though, having judged many a baking competition since, I don't blame them. Some entrants do seem to be somewhat lacking in personal hygiene, and there's nothing worse than when someone with a mucky fingernail offers you a slice of cake. The feedback seemed positive. I can't remember what they said, but I remember knowing I'd done well.

After that, we had to bake in a professional kitchen. We were given a recipe of Mary's this time, for a coffee and walnut cake, which we had to bake within a certain timeframe. My oven wasn't working, but I only realised after the cakes had gone in. Mary, bless her, crouched down and stuck her hand in my oven to see if it was warm. I panicked, but the producers gave us all an extra ten minutes or so, and I shoved my cakes into someone else's oven.

I went home thinking I'd royally messed up, but within a few weeks, they rang to say I was in the final thirty applicants. They just needed a few character references and for me to undergo an informal chat with a psychologist. I assumed that was to make sure we were all fit for the pressures of competition, but I've since come to realise that it is due diligence, ensuring reality television contributors can cope with the media interest, the potential press invasion and the painful thud when you inevitably fall, twice as fast as you climbed, from the dizzying heights of showbusiness and fame.

★ ★ ★

When Good Friday came, I was in Bristol ready to film the first episode. The minibus jumped over a humpback bridge as the *Bake Off* tent came into view. Our phones were taken away from us on arrival – so we couldn't cheat or take pictures to sell to the press – and away we went. I couldn't believe the scale of the production: there were people with cameras everywhere, runners, researchers, producers; there was a massive crane with a camera attached to it; there were make-up artists, touching up the faces of the judges and the presenters, Mel and Sue. The whole thing evoked the same feeling I'd experienced behind the scenes in theatres: a frantic, excited and nervous energy; an understanding that this huge spectacle would not be possible without each and every one of these people.

We'd film each episode of the competition at the weekend,

down in Bristol. During the week, I'd be back up in Manchester, revising for my final exams. I don't know what propelled me through it all. While it was, of course, stressful, I seemed to be in a focused and impenetrable trance. I've always maintained that having the two very different things to focus on meant my attention was never rooted in or obsessively niggling away at just one of them. If I started to feel an anxiety about the competition, I'd stick my face in an intellectual property law textbook. And if the Sale and Supply of Goods Act all got a little heavy, I'd practise my bakes. On Friday nights, back in Bristol with the rest of the bakers, we'd get totally pickled down by the docks on bottles of prosecco. I got on with most of the gang – when you're in such a condensed and unique scenario with strangers, that thing you all have in common, that one-of-a-kind-ness, brings you all together.

There were a couple of competitors I couldn't stand. I won't mention their names – what's the point? It was over ten years ago, and I'm sure they've changed as people, just as I have – but I felt that they were entitled and abrupt, rude and hurtful in their comments. I took a deep satisfaction in quietly and calmly knocking them off their high horses and waving them goodbye as they were eliminated. I was always tempted to say something unkind, but I knew better than that. Besides, cruel words only undress us, showing just how damn ugly we are inside. I refused to fire off missiles, because I'd only be hurting myself, my integrity. And I mustn't forget that we are all vulnerable creatures who react in uncharacteristic ways when under extreme pressure. I didn't know those people from Adam, so I certainly can't summarise their full personalities based on a few brushes with them. When we knock someone down, we don't stand any taller. Just rise above it, focus on yourself and move on.

It was all heavy going, but that was equalled – if not outweighed – by the fun we had. Although I was twenty-three, I still had that youthful air of nonchalance about me. By then, I'd felt the bitter sting of the disappointment of others, but here I felt emboldened and courageous. Their low opinions of me were *their* problem, not mine. I wanted to soak in every moment of joy I could: drinks on the harbour, the stress of the competition, the fulfilment I got from revising for my exams from the reams of lecture notes I had handwritten, typed up, added to and retyped over the course of my degree. I worked damn hard; I *always* work hard on anything I want to work hard on. And I'll forever have that to be proud of.

I couldn't have got through it, though, without Paul's support. Emotionally, he was constantly available, of course, but financially, he was a lifeline. He bought me a KitchenAid stand mixer when I got into the competition – an almond-cream-coloured one from the Peter Maturi kitchen shop in Manchester. I named it Melanie-Sue Berrywood after the presenters and judges. She was a buxom gal from the Deep South and knew how to whip together any dessert I needed. Despite being on a very basic wage, Paul knew how passionate I was about this, and how important it was for me to practise. Towards the end of the competition, while on a day out in Clitheroe, I begged him to buy me a huge pie dish that I needed for my American pie for pie week. It was eye-wateringly expensive for a piece of moulded aluminium, and when Paul asked if it was entirely necessary, I replied, 'This pie dish will pay for our future.'

We still laugh about that today, because in a small way, it has.

Only a select handful of people knew I was in the competition. I don't think I told my dad. I hardly saw him much by this point. We hadn't fallen out or anything, but distance had just weaved its way between us, and I can't recall how we had both let that happen.

* * *

On the Monday after the semi-finals of the competition, I sat my final exam – insurance law, I think. For my penultimate exam, intellectual property, I'd had to have extra time because my finger was bandaged after I cut it open on a food processor.

It was dessert week, and we were making strudel. Paul Hollywood was sitting at the table in the corner, where the judges had their conflab, and I was certain he was staring me out – undressing me with his eyes, as I like to say, to amuse crowds at food festivals. I'm sure he wasn't, but he was certainly intimidating. I found most straight men intimidating, to be honest. I just didn't know how to deal with them. I always feared that my presence, as a gay man, might be something they found uncomfortable and unlikeable. I found myself tempering who I was whenever I met a bloke, purposefully dulling my sparkle.

Drastically hungover from a night out with Cathryn – the friendly young mum in the competition, who was so super talented but just didn't believe it – I decided to give Paul a smile as I stuck my hand into the food processor to retrieve my strudel dough. The sharp scratch of the blade and that devastating feeling of separating skin jolted me – the feeling that screeches through your body, jangles your nerves and rings in your ears. I looked down to see blood pouring from my finger. The production team ushered me to a table and sat me down, instructing me to keep my hand above my head. Sue Perkins rushed over and grabbed my hand, squeezing the wound with blue roll. A member of the team told her to be careful of my blood. I assumed this was because of HIV, and then Sue confirmed that she had also understood it this way: 'I've worked with enough HIV patients to know about the risks,' she said.

I was grateful for her comfort and kindness. I don't know why the team member was concerned – was it health and safety, subtle homophobia, or a mix of the two? It doesn't matter; Sue was there.

After the final exam, that was it. Two years of dropping out, three years of hard work later, and my university education was over. With the final in sight, I put my foot to the floor and spent hours perfecting my final bake, the cake that would see me lift that glass cake stand (which, by the way, my mum claimed and has since broken – by accident!): the Heaven and Hell cake. It was a 30cm chocolate and orange chiffon cake, filled and covered with chocolate ganache, which I scraped absolutely smooth. Covered in a chocolate mirror glaze (which I used a hairdryer to level out) with a mountain of lemon and coconut cakes on top, it was truly my defining masterpiece. Everything until that point had been a bit hit or miss, as I'd let the competition get to my head. Here, in the final, I just harnessed that impenetrable trance-like focus and got on with it.

I didn't realise it at the time, but I was navigating the pathway of separation from my parents in a doubly concentrated way. Going to university is often what pushes young people to fly the nest. It's at this age and time that they become independent: surer of their political standpoints; forced to nourish and feed themselves, and manage their own finances. I was navigating that reality privately at university, but I was also doing it very publicly, in this big white circus tent. Had I realised that at the time, I think I would have been utterly derailed. It would have added an unscalable mountain of pressure.

We filmed the final in summer 2012, so I had a good three months before it was broadcast on BBC Two. During that purgatory, when I wasn't able to tell anyone – except, of course, Paul and my parents, sisters and grandparents – I didn't know where life would take me. Yes, I'd won the competition, but I had no idea what the public's reaction would be. Talent shows like that churn people out. Many of them are forgotten.

At my grandfather's funeral in August of that year, I got the results of my degree: a Bachelor of Laws, first class honours. I took the call from my university friend, Nikki, who had logged into my student portal to find out so she could tell me over the phone. I walked back inside, already clutching a large glass of wine to drown sorrows and celebrate life at the wake. I told my mum and stepdad, who were sitting at a crowded table with their friends. They all cheered, and Mum cried out, 'A year of heaven and hell indeed!'

We had champagne, but we never, ever clinked our glasses. We never do that in our family – ever since a cousin was killed in a car accident the night his parents were celebrating with champagne, my mum has insisted that we never let our glasses touch. That magical thinking was only amplified when my grandfather suffered his aneurism a day or two after we celebrated my *Bake Off* win – we didn't even need to clink glasses this time; it seemed that merely revelling in celebration was enough to take a life.

Just before the show aired, I started my graduate training scheme with the Royal Bank of Scotland. I didn't enjoy a moment of it – except the piss-ups with the other graduates – but, ever worried about a secure future, I just did it. As the competition aired, I started to feel a deep-rooted anxiety. People approached me in the streets and in bars, asking for photographs and autographs. It was lovely, and they were so kind, but it's an extremely unusual thing to get used to – fame. The one thing I was grateful for was that it was fame based on a widespread interest in food and baking. People wanted to ask me about the cakes and the competition; they weren't fawning over *me*, which I think was a really positive thing. Had they been there solely to bolster my ego, I think it would have all gone to my head a little more than it should have.

My anxiety levels came to a crunch when biscuit week was broadcast. I was especially tense. I knew this was the week that I admitted to having a boyfriend on camera, although I wasn't sure if it would make the final cut. As we watched it, there it was. I had said something along the lines of: 'My boyfriend Paul is a designer who works for an architectural firm, so he made the template.'

I headed straight to Twitter to see what the reaction was. Almost entirely warm and welcoming. The vast majority of commentators celebrated my coming out with such love. Paul and I both felt a little overwhelmed at how acceptable it seemed – how acceptable *we* seemed – to over seven million viewers.

The wider world seemed kinder than I'd expected.

★ ★ ★

Despite the understandable anxiety, it was mostly an exciting time. I was receiving so many freebies: champagne hampers in the post, meals out, holidays, even. It was all a twenty-three-year-old could have wanted. Life really changed, though, when my book proposal started to do the rounds with different publishers. I ended up taking part in what's known as a 'beauty parade'; my literary agent and I spent a day or two in London, going from office to office to meet editors at different publishing houses. In one of the last meetings I had, with Headline, the marketing manager – who is still a friend today – almost killed my agent, as he choked on an edible silver ball on the cake she had made. My dark sense of humour told me that this was a sign – a foreshadowing choking hazard – and within a couple of days, a six-figure offer was on the table. I was on platform one at Euston station when my agent gave me the news. Six figures, at twenty-three years old. I started to work out how long that would last me if all my other work dried up. I divided it by £12,000 (which I figured I could live off a year). I didn't clink a champagne glass, that's for sure. I felt afraid. If an income stream didn't continue, I would fail at this career – yet another disappointment.

A few days later, I told my boss at work that I was going to defer a year – a common theme in my career. He was so incredibly supportive. He and his wife were big fans of the show, so he appreciated the opportunity I had. He told me that if I didn't go for it now, I'd regret it.

When the final was aired, I watched it with my family and a huge gathering of friends at my mum and stepdad's house. As my name was announced and Mum's reaction was caught on camera, as she hugged me and cried, 'My little boy!', I realised there and then that her trying to control me going to Oxford wasn't out of anything other than her wanting the very best for me. She wanted me to be safe and happy, successful and secure. What she clearly hadn't realised until that point was that I could achieve all those things by myself. That I had to do it alone, in fact, because that made those achievements more meaningful and solid. A prestigious university education, to her, was the only way to achieve success. I think because I was the first of her family to go to university, it carried a particular weight.

My education didn't stop after law school, because I was also given a scholarship to study a diploma in pastry at the prestigious Le Cordon Bleu on Bloomsbury Square in London. I'd mentioned on the show that I wanted to study there, so the manager invited me in and offered me a scholarship worth over £15,000. I accepted with gratitude. People asked why I felt the need to study after I'd just won the most popular baking competition on television. I wanted to study because I wanted to be a professional, not just a home baker. I wanted, one day, to have my own cookery school or bakery, and to do that, I felt I needed a qualification. I didn't want to rest on my laurels – I wasn't yet good enough.

★ ★ ★

What surprised me most about life after *Bake Off* is that it didn't drastically affect my relationship with my partner, Paul. When I got the place at Le Cordon Bleu, we had to move down to London. While it was a big transition for us both, it was something we'd often thought about. And the jobs were better for him down there, anyway. He got a job with a trendy design agency in Old Street, and we rented a room from a friend's mum for a few months, before Paul – whose number-one hobby is trawling properties on Rightmove – found a fairly cheap flat for sale in Woolwich. With the money I had earned, we managed to buy it, and before even a year had passed, we were camped out in our first home together, eating pizza and watching films. We slept on the floor that night, and although it had been something I'd done a thousand times growing up, this time, I wasn't riddled with fear or anxiety. I was fuelled by love and excitement.

I tried to include Paul in everything I could, because neither of us had any friends in London. If I was invited to an event, I'd insist on a plus-one or decline the invitation. It wasn't that we were trying to cling on to one another in an unhealthy way; we just enjoyed each other's company. As we sat at the *Attitude* magazine awards, in a room full of celebrities in black tie, I was grateful to have him there with me. Together we wondered if one day I'd do anything award worthy.

We made so many wonderful new friends in the years after the show, meeting people from a diverse and broad range of careers. That's certainly one thing the exposure from a show like *Bake Off* brings: interest in you. People from all walks of life were interested in getting to know me. Some of them were fleeting opportunists – woodworms – but others have become friends for life. I never thought I'd come to share a bathtub with a Radio 4 newsreader and continuity announcer, but after becoming great friends, Susan Rae and I took a little trip to Richard Bertinet's cookery school in Bath, where we also treated ourselves to a trip to a spa at Babington House. The bath was big enough for two, so we weren't sitting awkwardly facing one another with our knees in our nostrils, but we still giggled about it for months to come. There was another evening, after some swanky party at an even swankier hotel, when we all got so pickled that Susan had to sleep in our room. We rang reception to bring up a folding bed, which arrived vertically and on wheels. We howled as Susan joked that she'd have to sleep upside down, strapped in like St Peter.

At Susan's Burns Night supper, Paddy O'Connell told me I had high-arched eyebrows like Angela Lansbury, just moments before he addressed the haggis. And there were drunken fondles and experiments with various soap stars and celebrities as Paul and I tested the boundaries of our relationship – though the details of those stories are perhaps for another volume.

But the icing on the cake had to be drinking tequila with two of the Spice Girls. Cleo Roccos, with whom I became pals through chocolatier Paul A. Young, had just recently launched her tequila brand, Aqua Riva, and so threw a throbbing (her words) launch party. We partied hard with them all, and I span around a coat stand with Richard Arnold – such a lovely chap. I can still taste the lime juice from throwing my guts up back at the flat in the early hours of that morning.

★ ★ ★

You might gather, from all the names I've just dropped in such a short space of time, that I got somewhat swept away with it all. After a while, I realised that I was spending a little too much of my money. *Bake Off* gave me wings, but I was beginning to fly a little too close to the sun, so as well as the investment in the flat, I decided it would be a good idea to set up a business. I didn't have a lot of money; people assumed I was a millionaire because I'd been on the telly, but that couldn't have been further from the reality. I'd already been teaching baking classes at a rented workshop in Greenwich, so knew there was a market for that. One of the first voices of authority I had met in the industry was Richard Bertinet, and he warned me about solely hopping from TV show to TV show – that just wasn't secure. He advised that I focus my attention on something more wholesome – the 'bread and butter', he called it. He'd done just that with his highly successful cookery school.

One of the barns on my stepdad's farm was out of use, filled only with Mum's pre-apocalyptic collection of bottles of Dettol, bagged-up pasta and rice, and cans of baked beans and tuna (she still hoards food in her cellar). My stepdad, who by this point seemed incredibly proud of me and my career, was so kind in helping me gut the barn. He renovated it, installing a new concrete floor and boiler, and I fitted it out with lighting, jazzy decorative tiles and kitchen workspaces. I used the contacts I had made since winning *Bake Off* to get sponsorships for things like ovens and KitchenAids, flour and sugar. The business proved to be immensely successful. People flew in from all over the world – Australia, New York, Germany – just to attend. I was always so overwhelmed that people would even want to make that journey to come to my little barn on the outskirts of Wigan. We were so busy with it that we sold our flat in Woolwich for a decent profit and bought a house up north. We'd always longed for a log fire and a dog; very soon, we had both. A friend in the pub had a springer spaniel who got a little carried away one night. We offered to take one of the unidentified mongrel puppies home, and we've loved him as our Abel ever since.

As well as writing my book, studying at pastry school, and setting up my own cookery school, I started to get offers for television work, which I accepted excitedly. I made countless pilots and had various screen tests, and I swiftly learned that my parents had been right about a career in performance: it is, indeed, a saturated market. As anyone in the industry will have experienced, there are more knockbacks than there are success stories. While that gives you a thick skin, it's easy to feel embittered by it all.

In the years after *Bake Off*, I started drinking more heavily than I ever had before. Part of that was due to hosting classes at my cookery school. Sometimes, the students would stay late into the evening, and the next day I'd find myself clearing away empty prosecco bottles. Sometimes, it was down to the industry gatherings, which were strewn with canapes and cocktails. I felt inferior, because I just didn't know what or where my voice was in the food industry at that time. I was aware that my entry into the sphere was via a glorified reality-TV show, so how could I ever compete with any of the big names? I felt so intimidated as I read Diana Henry and Yotam Ottolenghi, Nigella Lawson and Nigel Slater. I hadn't yet found my own tone of voice. I tried sometimes to be too posh – with both words and ingredients – and was scared of admitting that I seriously love a fish-finger sandwich with lashings of brown sauce, or even a Domino's pizza on the odd occasion. I thought that truth would undermine who I was. I felt like an imposter; an imperfect cog in a seemingly perfect machine, and I strived so hard to be exactly like the rest of them. But at events like the Fortnum and Mason awards, I had to down the drinks to confidently splash in the sea of chatter.

It wreaked havoc with my bulimia. As I tested recipes for my book, I found myself slumped over the toilet, often twice a day. I was most commonly triggered when a bake went wrong – which can still sometimes be the case today.

The problem with perfectionism is that it comes from the outside rather than the inside. Perfectionism is, for the most part, about measuring up to the perceived standards and expectations of others. The more I compared myself with these other food writers and television chefs, the more I convinced myself that I was a failure, never to be like them.

★ ★ ★

Much of it, though, was down to me wanting to self-destruct. I was so disheartened sometimes about projects not coming to fruition, and that would often turn to anger. As a result, I started to alienate some friends, by getting too drunk at parties and saying inappropriate or hurtful things. For a while, I had a weekly job on a morning TV show as one of its resident chefs. I was halfway through my contract, and had just got a mortgage on a house, when they decided to change the format. My job came to an abrupt end. I was both battered and furious. A year or so later, drunk and loose-lipped, I tweeted about how hypocritical the show was for having had me on talking about depression and mental health, before firing me within a couple of months of sharing that vulnerability. I took it personally, because, for me, it was personal.

It took me a while to get over that feeling of having been betrayed. The younger side of me, petulant and temperamental, had to learn what the industry is about. Of course, it is about celebrating personalities and their talents, but, for the most part, it is about selling headlines to promote the show, to keep the viewing figures up, to sell advertising space. It is a circus: a great spectacle that pulls a profit. That doesn't mean that the content within that circus is necessarily superficial or exploited, although it can be. Arguably, without that business-like approach, the content might not ever be given a platform to exist in the first place. Any business is the same: whether selling cakes, making movies or acting in the theatre, there is always a customer, always a service or product, and there are always sacrifices to be made. When you fall to the ground and scrape your knees, you have a choice. You can brush yourself off, stick a plaster on the wound and move on, or you can waste your energy shouting at the pavement.

I'll forever be grateful, though, for the fact I talked about my depression in that interview, because so many people wrote to me to tell me how much it helped them. Mental health is secretive, shameful, so speaking openly about it is a remedy. But I was also thankful for something a Twitter troll said: 'He's not depressed, he's just another wannabe celeb going through an identity crisis.' At first – for years, in fact – I brushed it off as an unnecessarily hurtful comment. For some reason, though, the remark resonated with me for quite some time. Looking back, it was so right, because I *didn't* know quite who I was. The troll was wrong about my depression – that was real and painful – but they were bang on the money with the identity part. And that was something I would need to figure out for myself.

Toffee Apple Upside-down Cake

───────

SERVES 12

This is one of the recipes that I designed as part of my application for *The Great British Bake Off*. I got my boyfriend to format it like a spread from a cookbook and had it printed on card. It's also the first recipe I baked on the show – the first challenge of the first day. It involves making a caramel, which is a simple process, but one that doesn't come without its potential pitfalls. Firstly, don't stir the sugar syrup once it is boiling, or it could crystallise – you can gently swirl the pan, but that's it. And most importantly, as soon as the caramel is a dark-amber colour, remove it from the heat and use as detailed – it sets solid very quickly. And please remember, caramel is ferociously hot and sticky, so avoid getting it on your skin at all costs.

For the toffee-apple topping
butter, for greasing
200g (7oz) caster (superfine) sugar
3 tablespoons water
3 large Granny Smith apples, peeled, cored and sliced into
1cm (½in) wedges

zest of 1 large orange
75g (2⅔oz) dried cranberries

For the cake
225g (8oz) Stork baking spread or butter, softened,
plus extra for greasing
225g (8oz) caster (superfine) sugar
2 teaspoons vanilla bean paste
225g (8oz) self-raising flour
½ teaspoon bicarbonate of soda (baking soda)
4 large eggs
60ml (4 tablespoons) full-fat milk

- Preheat the oven to 180°C/160°C fan/350°F/gas mark 4. Grease a 23cm (9in) square baking tin with butter and line it with baking paper (parchment paper).

- For the topping, place a saucepan over a high heat. Add the sugar and water and heat until the sugar melts and turns into an amber caramel – do not stir at any point. Remove from the heat and carefully pour it into the lined baking tin, taking care to cover the base completely. Arrange the apple wedges in three rows on top of the caramel and sprinkle with a third of the orange zest. Add the cranberries in any gaps between the rows of apple.

- For the cake, beat the baking spread or butter in a bowl with the remaining orange zest, along with the sugar and vanilla, until pale and fluffy – you can do this with a handheld electric mixer or using a stand mixer.

- In a separate bowl, sift together the flour and bicarbonate of soda. Add 1 tablespoon of this to the butter mixture, along with the eggs. Beat until combined, then add the rest of the dry ingredients and mix, just until you have a smooth batter. Stir in the milk.

- Pour the batter into the cake tin, over the caramel-apple layer, and gently smooth with a spatula. Bake for 40–50 minutes, or until a skewer inserted into the centre comes out clean.

- Once the cake has baked, and before it cools, use oven gloves to place a cooling rack over the tin and quickly flip it over, taking care not to burn yourself on any hot caramel that may leak from the tin. Remove the cake from the tin and set aside to cool completely. Serve in slices (it's lovely with a dollop of crème fraîche). This will keep for the best part of a week in an airtight container.

6.
Call of the Wild

———

Fight or flight is an instinct that lives within us all. Whether we choose to run away in the face of adversity or stand our ground and kick back is part of our genetic make-up, but also our upbringing. I guess it's less of a choice and more of a compulsion – and I am certainly compelled to flee. For some reason, I always long to migrate somewhere remote, to a place of extreme wilderness. As I've learned to know myself better, I've realised this is a way of cutting myself off from the bullshit. In my career – well, in most careers, I guess – there's an awful lot of figurative bullshit, but what I want is the *real* bullshit: the kind that fills the air with its potent pong and affronts the senses.

You too might be one of those people who scours the web for cabins deep in the forest or finds themselves in an online scroll-hole of videos about the people who have managed to live mortgage-free in a trailer house – tiny houses, as they're also cutely named. Sometimes I don't even realise I'm in the midst of a depressive episode until I have a sort of out-of-body experience and see myself motionless on the bed, staring at video after escapist video on YouTube. There's something fearsome about changing the status quo, reinventing the narrative. There's a discomfort that comes with travel, and adventure makes us porous – open to new things outside of the claustrophobic comfort we cling to.

The compulsion has got stronger as I've aged. I think one of the childish hopes we have is that as we get older, our feelings will wane, but I've found that the feelings I need for my own survival have got stronger, louder and harder to ignore. When I went back to law in 2018, aspiring to become a family-law barrister after my TV career had taken a downturn, I felt like I was on a healthy track to a decent future, moving towards the security that I had craved since I was a child. I crammed in so much work experience. I even shadowed a High Court judge. For a week or so, I followed him round from court room to court room, listening to the devastating details of a case involving a dead baby. As I sat down to a posh dinner with him and a High Sheriff, I asked how the latter could reasonably align his sexuality with his Catholic religion. The judge spat his cocktail out. 'That's a very direct question for so early on in the meal!' he laughed.

When I told Paul, he found it hilarious but wasn't at all surprised. 'You've never been one to make small talk about the weather.'

I was focused. I knew if I could get through a tough year of examinations, find a pupillage within chambers and shed the skin I'd developed from my TV years, I'd be fine.

But life had other plans, and I found myself bedbound with pneumonia. I didn't know I even had pneumonia until long after it had passed. I'd been to the hospital for an X-ray after my GP had given me antibiotics for a chest infection. It was only months later, when I saw a different doctor at the surgery to start a course of antidepressants, that he told me I'd had pneumonia. Either way, regardless of the time of diagnosis, the effects themselves meant I had to miss a chunk of my lectures, and I found it impossible to keep up. That catapulted me into a pit of depression. I'd already had to fight with the Bar Standards Board to reinstate my 'stale' law degree – I'd graduated six years earlier, and a law degree is only valid for a barrister training course for five. I'd already spent most of my savings, and I felt the weight of failure like concrete blocks around my feet as I stood on the edge of a cliff.

With that came thoughts of suicide. I'd lie awake at night, worried about my future, and from nowhere, the idea of hanging myself in the attic would arise. The scary thing about such feelings is how remarkably mundane they were – they just became part of my everyday pattern of thinking: wash the clothes, make dinner, kill yourself. I'd felt similar impulses before, when my relationship with my first boyfriend was falling apart. That's my problem: I allow emotional states to become all-consuming. It's difficult for me to regulate emotion and rationalise with myself. Suicidal thoughts sometimes seem to be my only way of coping.

My therapist at the time told me it was as though I always had that in my back pocket. No matter how shitty life could get, I always had the option to press the big red button on my existence.

My life *wasn't* shitty, though; that's the thing I struggled with. I had the world at my feet. I'd had a decent upbringing; I had a boyfriend who gave me more respect and love than I'd ever known; but still I felt empty because of my professional circumstances.

My therapist would say, 'No matter how hard life gets, remember that you've already been through the worst.'

'Bullshit,' I would think to myself. Because what had I actually been through? Divorced parents? An old-fashioned stepdad? An irregular relationship with my biological father? Yes, these things had proved to be challenging, but compared to growing up in crippling poverty or at the mercy of emotional or physical abuse, my life was a walk in the park. Yet the idea of suicide still haunted me.

But I knew I didn't want to die. I didn't want to leave behind my beautiful life: Paul, my family, my friends, my dog Abel. What I did know was that I needed to flee, to migrate to somewhere remote and do something repetitive, something basic, almost primal. For me, it was either the call of the wild or the call of the void. I chose the wild. I wanted to step into the cold air and feel alive, to contradict the dullness with which the sertraline – the antidepressant – was filling my life. Because it had started to replace my joy with numbness, and that was something I couldn't abide.

* * *

A friend had told me about WWOOF (Worldwide Opportunities on Organic Farms), an international organisation that links you to farms that need help. In return for physical labour, you get bed and board, but that's the only guarantee. Whether or not you'll gel with the host farmer or farming family is in the lap of the gods.

The first farm I looked into was a Buddhist tree-growing farm. The rules seemed strict: no phones, no alcohol, no sex. On one level, these restrictions appealed to me – could I challenge myself not to scroll through Instagram and not to drink myself into oblivion, as I all too often did? But what proved uncomfortably curious was that I didn't seem to be able to contact an owner or boss. Every form of correspondence I had regarding this place was with another Wwoofer, as though the person at the top was evading responsibility – or a paper trail. While I wanted a challenge, I certainly didn't want to end up slain and buried beneath the snow by some horticultural cult.

So I abandoned that idea and instead elected to work on a smallholding in Barriere, British Columbia, Canada, owned by Angela and Dan. A couple of years before, I'd been to Banff, Alberta, for a winter trip with Paul, and we'd both loved it. The snowy, ragged mountains looked like they were torn from paper, and vast forests, dusted with icing sugar, sprawled across the landscape. The magnitude of the place is so humbling, it makes you realise how insignificant you are as an individual. At any moment, you could get lost in a snowstorm, fall into a frozen lake or be attacked by a cougar or bear. That rarely happens, I know, but who's to say it couldn't? But it isn't just the physical threats of a place like this that dwarf us; it's the sense of time, too. We see our lives as deep and meaningful, but against the backdrop of this ancient horizon, they stand shallow and minor. Temporary. The mountains will not remember our names after we have turned to dust. That appealed to me.

I told my mum I was going, and she begged me not to. She wanted me to finish my barrister course, to follow it through. I could see the disappointment in her eyes. She misinterpreted this as me running away from life, when actually I was running towards it. I don't blame her, because that is, of course, what it looked like. But I knew that if I stayed, I wouldn't make it out alive. Paul, I think, knew that too. He worried I was fleeing him for a little while, but I did my best to reassure him. I promised him I knew what I was doing, and that I'd return refreshed and renewed. I didn't know this for sure, and a little part of me was also scared that maybe the consistency of a relationship was too much for my short attention span. Maybe the twelve or so years we had been together was all too regular and repetitive, and I needed to seek a more sporadic thrill.

But I also knew that the security I had with Paul was something I needed, something I valued and longed for. I've been a butterfly all my life; I pick up interests and work on them intensely, then get bored. Then the boredom turns to erratic decision-making, or wild nights out where I get so pissed I finally stop thinking, or episodes of bingeing on so much food that I have to force it out of me.

Surely a little hard work on a Canadian farm was better than any of that?

Within days of finding the farm, I'd booked a flight to Vancouver, filled a rucksack with winter clothes, shaved my head so I could focus on just waking up and working and set off for the Canadian wilderness. I spent a night in Vancouver, where I met a friend, Nicole – ironically one of the first people I'd worked with in television after winning *Bake Off.* She had been a producer at Food Network, for which I'd made a few programmes, and she and I had really hit it off. For some reason or another, she had left the TV world and moved back home to Canada to be with her mother. We sat in a bar and ate poutine (chips, gravy and cheese curds) and drank Caesar cocktails (a kind of Bloody Mary, made with Clamato – a clam and tomato juice drink).

The next morning, I woke early and headed to the bus station. Under the weight of my rucksack, I actually felt lighter. I knew I was doing the right thing for me, despite Mum's concerns and Paul's worries.

I chuckled as I thought about Nicole shouting, 'I believe in Tim Stephens!' (a Canadian astrologer) when I asked her if she believed in astrology. We had been talking about star signs; I am always so intrigued by people's belief in them. When I was younger, I had wanted to be a witch; so much so that I watched Disney's *Sleeping Beauty* every single morning, and begged my sisters to make me magic wands. In primary school a couple of my girlfriends and I started dabbling in spells, which we'd download off the internet and print out. Before I went on a family holiday to Gozo one year, I cast an anti-bullying spell on a lad who had tormented me for years. I gathered rose petals and candles in the toilet on the farm, and whispered some laborious incantation I'd found. I went away, thinking nothing of it, but on my return it turned out the lad had been expelled from school. I was convinced it was thanks to the spell, but it transpired that he'd merely had a week of bad behaviour, and the straw that broke the donkey's back was him farting on purpose. I wasn't powerful; he was just disruptively gassy.

I remember dressing as a witch for Halloween, way before we had left my first home and moved to the farm. Already concerned that I wasn't like the other lads on the estate, Mum's response was: 'Boys are warlocks, not witches.' Clearly, I was more effeminate, more interested in wigs and high heels than the other boys on the estate – I used to wear her boob tube as a dress around my tiny body. I loved the clattering sound her high heels made on the tarmac, as I shuffled about in them. I don't think she was in any way ashamed of me, but I could tell she was worried and wanted to protect me. I imagine she'd seen the hateful things done to queer people in the 70s and 80s. But it didn't matter where her concerns sat; I interpreted comments like that as dissatisfaction with the boy I was, and that certainly kissed the ever-increasing shame within me. Despite her worries, she didn't prevent me from dressing as, or having an interest in, witches. I remember standing on one the worktops in the kitchen – I must have been five or six – and finding a Halloween cartoon book all about witches on top of the fridge, which she'd stashed away as a present for me.

But Nicole shouting that in the bar, warmed and pink from the Caesars, reminded me of that magical thinking I had clung to as a child. And as I ploughed my way through the snow that morning, I realised I continue to think in that childish way sometimes. I'm always overwhelmed by the beauty of snow, the way it makes everything equal and seemingly brings everything together. It blankets the prejudice and separation in the natural world. To this day, as soon as the first snowflakes begin to fall, I worry about the day they'll melt. I can't just sit and enjoy them while they last, but instead panic about their future, about the sun reappearing and melting them to a dirty, dull mush. I could live in a winter wonderland for ever.

* * *

That innocent thinking was soon forced out of my head, as the bus to Kamloops sped through the ice and snow. The Coquihalla Highway is a white-knuckle ride, and it was probably the scariest bus journey I'd ever been on. It forced me to think about my college friend Rebecca, who'd died in a bus crash in Ecuador while on her gap year, ten years earlier. At her funeral, her father decided not to read a eulogy, but instead to give the speech he would have given at her wedding, and the entire church – filled beyond capacity with people who loved her – froze with emotion.

In the pews of this hurtling bus, I closed my eyes and let the tears stream as I drifted off. Was I a disappointment to my family? Was I really just that butterfly who couldn't hold anything down, who had simply been lucky with my career and hadn't actually worked hard for it? When I pictured my own father and imagined him giving the same kind of speech Rebecca's father had given, I couldn't breathe. That was a pain I hadn't yet processed.

I woke up in Kamloops to be met by Dan, the elderly farmer, who then drove me in his truck the hour or so to his farm in Barriere. It was a strained journey, as the engine was loud and he was a little deaf, so everything I said needed to be repeated at increased volume. I don't think he understood my deep Lancashire accent, either. Added to this was the fact that I still didn't interact well with men outside the group of friends I had learned to trust. Because of my past, I feared them, and would practically roll over like an overly submissive dog. I'd started to notice that the way I interacted with men was very different from the way I interacted with women. I was comfortable around women, able to be myself. But around men, I'd present myself with bravado, even speak in a deeper voice. Men were my captors. Women, so far, had set me free.

Dan's pure-white hair glistened in the low winter sun, and his clear skin and piercing blue eyes spoke of a healthy life. I soon learned that pretty much everything he and everyone else on the farm ate, aside from butter and milk and breakfast cereal, they either grew or reared themselves, and what they harvested during summer and autumn was kept in the root store over winter.

Giant logger trucks whirred past us as we made our way along the highway into the mountains. Everything was covered in snow, and some of the trees stood black and imposing, as though drawn from charcoal by L. S. Lowry. I later learned they'd been burned several years previously in a fierce fire started by a cigarette; the flames had been so violent they had even jumped across the river. Homes had been destroyed, and the blaze had cost over 30 million Canadian dollars to extinguish.

As I got out of the van in the early-evening darkness and breathed in the scent of the woodfire outside the garage that heated the entire house, I heard animal footsteps in the snow getting louder as something charged towards me. Dan had already told me to be mindful of coyotes and cougars, and also that there were wolves further up in the mountains, as well as grizzly bears, though they were most likely deep in hibernation. I winced as something large and furry hit my legs. Dan saw my face and chuckled as he introduced me to Luke, the huge white Italian Maremma dog that patrolled the farm at night and guarded the sheep from predators. For such a large beast, Luke was the softest and most loving creature. Every night, when I let him off his lead to patrol the farm, he'd press his giant head into my lap and roll over for belly rubs. Every morning, I'd shout for him to come for his breakfast, so I could attach him to the lead and release Cheyenne, the older Rottweiler cross, but Luke would hide. Eventually, I got to know where to find him, and had to drag him from beneath the deck of the house by his collar as he grumbled at me. I was, of course, well used to dragging feral animals from beneath furniture and buildings, having lived with feral cats back on my own farm as a lad.

The farmers were impressed with my fearlessness when it came to dogs – many of the other Wwoofers had been seriously afraid – especially when I had to carry Cheyenne into the house after she lost the use of her legs because of an infection. Dan was surprised she didn't snap at me – as dogs often do when in pain – but I knew we had established a relationship of trust. I'd fed her, played with her, stroked her; I'd even laid down in the snow and given her a cuddle. I trusted her. She trusted me.

Working with the animals made me think a lot about the relationships we have as humans. Too often, they become complicated and muddied with psychology and fear, when really all we need to do is love and listen, nourish and nurture. That's how Paul had treated me over the years, despite my destructive behaviour and early possessiveness. He'd listened to me and accepted I was flawed; he'd tamed me – a frightened, feral dog – and he'd done it all with a non-judgemental love.

★ ★ ★

My first duty was to see to the chickens. I had to fill their feeders with grain and water, then collect the eggs in a white bucket. Sometimes, the hens would still be sitting in their boxes, and as I slid my hands beneath their warm, fluffy bodies, they'd peck at me. They never drew blood, but it did sometimes hurt. After a while, I learned to stroke their bills with one hand while I retrieved the eggs with the other, and they got to know that I wasn't an enemy. I'd then leave the bucket of eggs on the porch of the house, and once I'd done all my other outside chores I'd go back and scrub them clean with dish soap and a nail brush down in the basement, box them up and store in the fridge.

After the hens, I'd drive the quadbike up to the cows. Overnight, the water in their drinking bathtubs would freeze and need breaking. Sometimes, the ice was fifteen centimetres thick, but I wasn't allowed to use anything other than my hands and a wooden pole. If I'd used a pickaxe – as I once suggested – I could easily have broken through the bathtub, so the only option was brute force and gritted teeth. Kash, the black calf, would come and lick my head every morning. Her sandpaper tongue kissed my forehead. It reminded me of the calves back home on the farm, and I felt a pride in that little lad who had moved to the farm in fear but carried on regardless. He had survived, just as I was choosing to do now.

On the way down from the cows, I'd call in to see the pigs and throw feed into their trough. I'd been warned never to climb into the pen with them, because they could – and probably would – eat me. They were bloody massive, and they'd snaffle their food as soon as it was flung over the fence. I heeded that warning, and never once dared to go in with them.

The job I could never get quite right was feeding the sheep. After trying – and often failing – to reverse the quadbike and trailer into the barn, I'd pitchfork hay into the trailer. Angela showed me how to pile it up and use the pitchfork to pin the mound together, like a hairpin through a tightly wrapped bundle of golden hair. But I'd always either put too little or too much on, and as I went through the gate into the field with the sheep, the fork would fly out and the hay would tumble to the ground. The sheep wouldn't politely wait for me to fork the hay back into the trailer, but would instead set to devouring it, impatiently pushing me out of the way. Tonto, a llama who was clearly going through an identity crisis and considered himself one of the herd, would almost snigger as I battled with fork and flock.

A lot of life on the farm was repetitive. Each morning, I'd wake up at six, make my bed and have coffee in the lounge with Dan and Angela, before carrying out the same farmyard chores. After the snow had fallen, I'd be outside with the shovel or the snow plough attached to the quad, clearing paths, tracks and doorways. The child in me questioned the point in repeating the same back-breaking work, when just hours later, the snow would return and we'd have to start again. But there was no way around it; the animals depended entirely on us for their survival, and if we didn't remove the fresh snow, it would freeze, meaning pathways would become lethal and barn doors would be jammed shut by berms of ice.

I'd never heard the sound of snowfall until this trip. Flakes the size of small crisps futtered to the ground, landing, more heavily than their volume suggested, with audible sighs of relief. It reminded me of Matthew Bourne's *Swan Lake*, and the way the male swan dancers exhale loudly together as they dance. But like beautiful swans, the snow was potentially dangerous. Treading through it became much easier as time went by, but for the first few days, Dan would be able to tell how many times I'd slipped and fallen over by counting my ass prints. He seemed concerned that I shouldn't injure myself, but at the same time, we both found it amusing.

* * *

My butterfly brain naturally found the repetition difficult, but the responsibility bore more weight than my impatience, and I impressed myself with the way I just got on with it. How quickly the childish thinking dissolved. I soon became a creature of habit, grateful for knowing what each day would have in store. I thought of the Buddhists who create intricate mandalas with coloured sand, only to later sweep and wash them away – a reminder that life itself is impermanent, everything is transient, and it's wrong to become too attached to anything or anyone. I wondered if my grandma completed then disassembled jigsaw puzzles with the same mindset. Was it just a way for her to pass the time, or was it a spiritual undertaking? Was there a difference? Was my old nan an enlightened being? She certainly looked entranced as she gobbled handfuls of jelly babies while plonked in front of *Loose Women*.

I started to appreciate the parallels between life on the farm in Canada and my childhood. As well as working on the farm, Angela was also a part-time nurse down in the town, so she was out during the day a lot, like my own mother, who had also been a nurse during my childhood. If she wasn't working in the chip shop or in the nursing home, Mum would be doing farm work or cooking dinner.

One day, Angela and I had to clean all the sheep's hooves and douse them in iodine, because of a foot fungus that had broken out on the farm. Angela asked me to hold the sheep's heads underneath their chins, but I'd learned at a young age that the best way to hold a sheep in place was to straddle it and hold its neck in between my thighs to stop it moving and bucking. Angela was impressed by this technique – something she'd never seen before – and I felt helpful and accomplished. As we worked together, scraping the hooves in the dim light of the barn, I was transported to the UK foot-and-mouth crisis, back in 2001.

Every winter, we'd look after sheep belonging to a Welsh farmer, because the conditions on the mountains were far too cold and dangerous for the flock during these months. Because movement of animals was banned during the outbreak, we had to keep the sheep in the barns longer than usual. Late at night and at first light, Mum and I would go into the barns with a torch to check the mouths of all the sheep, looking for any signs of the disease. I remember the panic on Mum's face if anything seemed irregular, but thankfully we avoided any infection.

I came to realise, on this snow-covered Canadian farm, 4,500 miles away from home, that although my childhood had indeed been dotted with some serious anxiety and loneliness, I had some beautiful and unique memories to reflect upon, too. After all, not many other children can say they've been up at 5am looking into sheep's mouths with a torch, nestled in the straw, under the dim yellow light of a single bulb.

My sheep-wrangling skills came in very handy a few times. Cole, the youthful and ballsy ram, would often escape the sheep pen with Tinkerbell, a devoted girlfriend who followed him wherever he roamed. One afternoon, Angela and Dan headed into town for a date night. As I was cleaning up after experimenting with a doughnut recipe made using mashed potatoes (Dan had specifically requested it as a blast from his past), I glanced out of the window and saw Cole and Tinkerbell tiptoeing across the farmyard like Bonnie and Clyde. Tea towel in hand and shoelaces untied, I somehow managed to herd them back into the wrong side of the barn, where the hay was stored. Once I'd slid the door shut, I had to find an old end of rope to make a noose and tie it loosely around their necks to guide them into the pen. Tinkerbell acquiesced, quite gracefully, and followed my instructions. Cole, on the other hand, kicked and headbutted me, knocking me to the floor and sending sheep food flying all over the place. I climbed on to the bale of hay to avoid his lashing out, then leapt on to his back and whipped the rope beneath his head. It was like riding a bucking bronco; I kept his shoulders and neck in between my legs and clamped on to him as he thrashed. Eventually, I managed to force him back into the pen, which I then tied up as tightly and intricately as I could. I remembered my grandad telling me: a sheep's only aim in life is to escape.

* * *

I had been worried about coming to conservative Canada – cowboy country – as an openly gay man. But I'd learned over the years, as most people within my community do, to play it either fairly straight, or so extravagantly camp that people think you own the world. But, to my surprise, I didn't have to deal with any bigotry here. Kieron, Angela's son, sometimes made jokes that were a little too close to the bone.

After I'd taken a shower once, he asked, in front of everyone, 'Did you wash the gay out of the tub when you were done?'

'I tried to,' I replied, 'but every time I bent over, glitter shot out of my ass.'

We all howled with laughter. I knew he wasn't being hateful, because we'd spent so much time alone together baking in the kitchen, or out in the yard, shooting at tin cans. He asked me openly and interestedly about Paul, and was never judgemental about my lifestyle. That was a common theme – people making jokes about my sexuality to prove how 'cool' they were with it. But perhaps we need to move on from that now. Perhaps I should have told Kieron that to accept someone's sexuality or gender is to stay silent or to proactively support it. It is never to chip away at it, even if just for humour's sake. But by the end of my time on the farm, he was making fewer jokes about my sexuality, and I think he realised he could be comfortable with it, without needing to make silly remarks to prove it. I would never hold that against someone who had already proven himself to be a decent person.

That's why cancel culture is such a pointless thing. Of course, if someone makes a hateful remark about a minority group, they should indeed be called out. But by cancelling someone, you stop the conversation dead. Mindsets cannot be changed, and opinions cannot be educated, if everything falls quiet and freezes deep beneath the snow. I sincerely believe that closing off the discussion is just an easy way to avoid confrontation. By fighting for our liberty, by having uncomfortable conversations, we can make changes; some tiny, some titanic. Democracies are founded on debate; justice in court rooms comes from adversaries each presenting their own version of events. Shouting down is simply autocracy or illiberal dictatorship – it is the action of an authoritarian wolf in sheep's clothing. We mustn't lose the power of debate, as painful as it may be to hear it.

★ ★ ★

I didn't drink much while on the farm, apart from the odd glass of rye, and a few beers one afternoon in the Barriere Motor Inn (known as the BMI) a few weeks after my arrival. But even after that small quantity I woke up the next day feeling snappy and moody. For the most part, I'd spend my evenings sitting on the porch in the darkness, wrapped in a blanket with Luke by my side, waiting with my camera to take photographs of the stars. Under the light of the moon, the snow glittered, and my eyes would fill with tears as the coyotes and wolves serenaded me from high in the mountains and stars showed off their fires. I'd never seen so many eyes staring back at me in the darkness, in both the sky and the fields. It was a world away from the flashing lights of nightclubs and endless fountains of liquor I would indulge in back home.

★ ★ ★

That trip to Canada taught me a great deal, but one of the things I am most grateful for is that it rekindled my love affair with food. After running a cookery school for a few years, where I'd cooked and baked for a living, the conversation with food got a little bit stale for me, and my bulimia made me afraid to enjoy food that wasn't within a regular and rigid routine and diet plan. On the farm, though, I'd need to cook lunches for Dan and me to enjoy together. Angela would make delicious soups – her chicken soup, a golden elixir that defrosted our cold bodies after a morning on the farm, was the best I've had – and cheese biscuits (scones to us Brits) to enjoy with stews. I found myself baking just for fun again, and I taught her how to make my cinnamon buns with bacon-fat cream-cheese frosting, which she'd take proudly into work to share with her colleagues.

Kieron and I spent a lot of time in the kitchen, too. He showed me how to make the Canadian classic, Nanaimo bars, and in return, I taught him to make fougasse and choux au craquelin. We used this pastry to make s'mores eclairs, filled with a chocolate crème pâtissière and topped with a marshmallowy Swiss meringue. Angela had to ask me to give the kitchen a rest at one point, because I was churning out cakes faster than Mr Kipling's factory. We were all getting a little rounder in the middle.

As I cared for the animals, baked cakes and pastries and cleared snowy pathways, and as I bore witness to the pitter-patter of falling snow in the deep and sacred silence, I no longer felt like taking my life. I felt like living it. Gently and with grace. I wasn't fleeing after all; I was very much fighting.

Salted Peanut Nanaimo Bars

———

MAKES 18

These are an adapted version of the recipe that Kieron gave to me on the farm in Canada. Normally, the base would include coconut, graham crackers and walnuts, but I've gone for a slightly different take on it. They're basically a no-bake refrigerator bar, and are so damn good after a morning of physical activity on a farm – though I'd happily take one after a short use of brain power while sat at my desk.

For the base
200g (7oz) unsalted butter, diced, plus extra for greasing
80g (2¾oz) cocoa powder
100g (3½oz) caster (superfine) sugar
2 large eggs
175g (6oz) digestive biscuits (graham crackers),
bashed to coarse rubble
175g (6oz) Hobnobs (oat cookies), bashed to coarse rubble
75g (2⅔oz) salted peanuts, roughly chopped
200g (7oz) chopped dates

For the peanut butter buttercream
200g (7oz) unsalted butter

100g (3½oz) smooth peanut butter
500g (1lb 2oz) icing (confectioners') sugar, sifted
2 tablespoons custard powder (like Bird's)

For the chocolate layer
400g (14oz) dark chocolate (55 per cent cocoa solids)
60g (2¼oz) unsalted butter, diced
75g (2⅔oz) salted peanuts

To decorate
edible bronze lustre powder
vodka or water

- First grease a 23 × 33cm (9 × 13in) baking tray and line as neatly as possible with non-stick baking paper (parchment paper). I like to put a strip of paper along the length of the tin, with excess overhanging at both ends, then repeat the other way, so the base and all four edges of the tin are lined. Secure the excess baking paper with small bulldog clips.

- For the base, put the butter, cocoa powder and sugar into a heatproof mixing bowl and set over a pan of simmering water. Stir until the butter melts and everything is combined. Still over the heat, add the eggs and whisk constantly to prevent them from scrambling, until the mixture feels hot to the touch.

- Remove the bowl from the heat and add the digestives, Hobnobs, peanuts and dates, then stir to mix everything well – the texture should be rather like rocky road. Tip the mixture into the tin and level it out with your hands or the back of a spoon to make sure it's evenly distributed over the entire base of the tin. Chill for at least an hour.

- When the base layer has chilled, make the buttercream. Beat the butter and peanut butter together in a mixing bowl with a handheld electric mixer until pale and fluffy. Add the icing sugar and custard powder, and slowly incorporate them into the butter mixture. Increase the speed and whip until very smooth and fluffy – this will take a good few minutes. Tip the buttercream on to the chilled base layer and spread out as evenly as possible, then freeze for an hour.

- After an hour, make the chocolate layer. Put the chocolate and butter in a bowl set over a pan of barely simmering water, stirring occasionally until they have completely melted, and the mixture is smooth and glossy. Quickly pour it over the cold buttercream and level off as evenly as possible with a small offset palette knife. Before the chocolate has a chance to set, sprinkle over the peanuts, then score it into 18 portions with a sharp knife – I do six scores across the width, and three along the length. Allow the bars to set in the fridge for 30 minutes before cutting. These are best cut with a very sharp knife dipped into a jug of boiling-hot water – be sure to carefully clean the blade between each slice.

• To finish, mix a little edible bronze lustre powder with vodka or water. Dip a clean toothbrush into the mixture, then pull the bristles back towards you and release them so the lustre sprays across the bars in beautiful splodges and splashes. These bars should keep for a week, if stored in an airtight container.

Maple Cinnamon Buns with Bacon Fat Frosting

MAKES 12

We ate so much bacon on the farm, because Angela and Dan had an abundant supply of it, made from their own pigs. Perhaps that's another reason they never went into the pig pen – so they didn't get too close or emotionally attached to the animals. The day I taught Angela to make these, she was so excited about taking them into work with her the next day. Nothing got wasted on the farm – leftover soup was made into bread, and I used the bacon fat to make these buns. To get enough bacon fat, put a pack of smoked streaky bacon (reserving two rashers for the candied topping) on to a baking sheet with a slight lip to catch the fat. Put that into a cold oven and set it at to 200°C/180°C fan/400°F/ gas mark 6. After about 15–20 minutes, the oven will have got hot, and in that time the fat will have rendered out of the bacon. I usually make enough for several batches of buns, pouring the fat I'm not using into little dip pots (saved from whenever we have an Indian takeaway), which I store in the freezer. The smokiness is key, so make sure you used smoked bacon.

For the dough
250g (9oz) plain (all-purpose) flour,
plus extra to dust
250g (9oz) strong white bread flour
7g sachet fast-action dried yeast
1 teaspoon fine sea salt
270ml (9¼fl oz) full-fat milk
50g (1¾oz) maple syrup
40g (1½oz) unsalted butter, diced
1 large egg
flavourless oil (like sunflower),
for greasing

For the filling
225g (8oz) unsalted butter, diced
100g (3½oz) light muscovado sugar
40g (1½oz) maple syrup
50g (1¾oz) plain (all-purpose) flour
3 tablespoons ground cinnamon
pinch of salt

For the candied bacon
2 rashers smoked streaky bacon, finely diced
2 tablespoons caster (superfine) sugar

For the frosting
40g (1½oz) soft unsalted butter

20g (¾oz) bacon fat from smoked streaky bacon
(optional – but so worth it)
125g (4½oz) full-fat soft cheese
60g (2¼oz) maple syrup

- To make the dough, put both flours, the yeast and the salt into the bowl of a stand mixer fitted with a dough hook.

- Combine the milk, maple syrup and butter in a saucepan and set over a high heat. As soon as the milk feels just warm, remove it from the heat – the butter won't have melted fully. Pour this mixture into the stand mixer, along with the egg. Knead on a medium speed for 7–10 minutes, or until very smooth and elastic.

- Shape the dough into a ball, add a glug of oil and turn the dough so it gets a good coating. Cover the bowl with a clean tea towel and leave the dough to prove until it has doubled in size. This should take around 1 hour, though it could be longer if your kitchen is cold – I take a 'before' photo on my phone to use as a comparison.

- Meanwhile, make the brown butter for the filling. Melt the butter in a saucepan over a medium heat. Then crank up the heat and bring to the boil, swirling the pan every 30 seconds or so. As the bubbling starts to quieten and a cappuccino-like foam appears on the surface, take off the heat and pour into a shallow dish to cool and solidify.

- When the dough has doubled in size, pop the bowl in the freezer for 15 minutes or so to firm it up a little, making it easier to roll out.

- Meanwhile, return to the filling. Add the sugar, maple syrup, flour, cinnamon and a good pinch of salt to the semi-set brown butter and stir to form a paste.

- Dust the worktop with flour and roll out the dough into a 45cm (18in) square. Spread the filling evenly over the square of dough, then roll it up into a very tight spiral. Trim the messy ends (I bake these on a separate tray as chef's perk), then cut the dough into 12 even portions. They will be large, but that is how they should be.

- Place the dough portions, spiral-side up, in a well-greased baking tin measuring 23 × 33cm (9 × 13in). Cover loosely with clingfilm (plastic wrap) and allow to prove until doubled in size – again, the time this will take could be anything from 45 minutes up, so keep an eye on them.

- For the candied bacon, set a small frying pan over a medium heat and add the chopped bacon. Cook gently, just until slightly browned. Add the sugar and, without stirring, allow it to melt into a pool of amber caramel. Now stir the caramel and the bacon together, just until the bacon is fairly evenly coated, then tip on to a piece of baking paper (parchment paper) to cool and set.

• When the buns have doubled in size, preheat the oven to 200°C/180°C fan/400°F/gas mark 6 and bake them for 15–20 minutes, or until lightly golden and cooked through.

• Meanwhile, make the frosting. Using a handheld electric mixer, cream together the butter and bacon fat in a bowl, then add the soft cheese, followed by the maple syrup, and continue mixing until the mixture is smooth and well combined.

• As soon as the buns come out of the oven, spread the frosting over them. Break the candied bacon into pieces and sprinkle it over the top. Cool for 10–15 minutes before eating. These are best eaten within two days of baking.

Chicken soup

———

SERVES 6, HEARTILY

Deep in the basement of the farmhouse, there was a huge chest freezer filled exclusively with meat reared on the farm. With the chicken offcuts and legs, and veg from the root store, Angela would make the most delicious chicken soups, which we'd savour as we cherished each minute of our lunchtime together. She never gave me the exact recipe, but this is my version, which I've made ever since.

1.5kg (3lb 5oz) chicken legs (bones in, skin on)
3 onions, roughly chopped
2 carrots, peeled and roughly chopped
1 parsnip, peeled and roughly chopped
3 celery sticks, roughly chopped
3 garlic cloves, crushed
4 fresh bay leaves
small handful of dried macaroni or pasta shells
bunch of flat-leaf parsley, finely chopped
small bunch of dill, finely chopped
juice of 1 lemon
2 teaspoons light brown muscovado sugar
salt and pepper

- Put the chicken into a large pot and add enough water to cover it by about 10cm (4in). Bring to a boil over a high heat, then reduce to a simmer and cook for 30 minutes or so, skimming off the foam and impurities that form on the top.

- Add the veg, garlic and bay leaves and return to the boil, then simmer for another hour, removing the foam and impurities as required.

- Next, remove the chicken with kitchen tongs (you can turn off the heat) and set aside on a tray until cool enough to handle, then shred the meat, discarding the bones and skin.

- Bring the broth back to a simmer and add the pasta. Cook for 10 minutes, or until tender, then add the herbs, lemon juice, sugar and salt and pepper to taste (I like plenty!). Stir in some of the shredded chicken meat (chill the rest for sandwiches and salads). If this makes too much soup for one sitting (which it inevitably will), you can keep it in the fridge for 3 days, or freeze it in batches for up to 3 months.

Store-Cupboard Beef Stew with Cheese Biscuits

————

SERVES 4

I made this for dinner one evening using the pressure cooker (which I actually used a fair bit during my stay at the farm). Here, I have adapted the recipe to be cooked slowly in the oven (or a slow cooker – though do please ensure you reduce it by boiling it until thickened if cooking it that way). Angela found it a little bit rich – her stews were much more delicate – but Dan and I certainly wolfed it down, with a batch of cheese biscuits Angela made to go alongside.

For the stew
600g (1lb 5oz) beef shin, diced
1 tablespoon plain (all-purpose) flour
2 tablespoons sunflower oil
1 onion, chopped
2 large carrots, cut into bite-sized chunks
a few sprigs of flat-leaf parsley, stalks and leaves separated,
finely chopped
2 star anise
2 fresh bay leaves
6 thyme sprigs
295g (10½oz) can condensed tomato soup

440ml (15½fl oz) can Guinness
1 beef stock cube, crumbled
350ml (12fl oz) water
salt

For the biscuits
225g (8oz) plain (all-purpose) flour
1½ teaspoons baking powder
40g (1½oz) unsalted butter, chilled, plus extra to serve
50g (1¾oz) Cheddar, grated
75g (2⅔oz) natural yogurt
75g (2⅔oz) half-fat crème fraîche
1 teaspoon lemon juice
1 egg, beaten, to glaze

- Preheat the oven to 160°C/140°C fan/325°F/gas mark 3 and line a baking tray with baking paper (parchment paper).

- In a bowl, toss the beef with the flour and a pinch of salt. Heat 1 tablespoon of the oil in a heavy-based casserole over a high heat. Brown the beef in batches until deep golden brown on all sides. Transfer to a plate and set aside.

- Heat the remaining oil in the same pan over a medium heat. Add the onion, carrots and chopped parsley stalks (reserve the leaves for the biscuits). Cook for about 10 minutes, or until the onion is softened, then add the remaining stew ingredients.

Bring to the boil, then return the beef to the casserole. Cover and cook in the oven, stirring occasionally, until the beef flakes apart and the sauce is rich and glossy – this should take around 3½ hours. Add a little water if it's looking too thick at any point.

- Half an hour before the stew is ready, make the biscuits. In a bowl, mix together the flour and baking powder, then rub in the butter with your fingers until the mixture resembles fine crumbs. Add a pinch of salt, along with the chopped parsley leaves and the Cheddar. Add the yogurt, crème fraîche and lemon juice and bring the mixture together into a dough. Cover and leave to rest for 20 minutes, then roll out on a floured surface to a disc about 2cm (¾in) thick. Cut this into eight wedges and arrange on the prepared baking tray. Glaze with the beaten egg.

- When the stew is cooked, remove from the oven and allow it to rest. Increase the temperature to 210°C/190°C fan/410°F/ gas mark 6½. Bake the biscuits for 20 minutes, or until golden brown and well risen, then transfer to a wire rack to cool for 5–10 minutes.

- Season the stew to taste, then serve with the biscuits on the side, slathered with butter.

Fougasse

———

MAKES 2

Kieron was already pretty good at making bread – how could he not be, when his mother, Angela, made such beautiful loaves? – but he was excited to learn how to make these. I've been making them since before *Bake Off*, since way back when I had a food blog at university. But even to this day, when I make them, all uneven and rustic, it feels like an accomplishment.

For the filling
knob of salted butter
1 red onion, finely sliced
1 teaspoon balsamic vinegar
1 teaspoon caster (superfine) sugar

For the dough
250g (9oz) strong white bread flour, plus extra for dusting
5g (⅛oz) salt
7g sachet fast-action dried yeast
2 rosemary sprigs (or another herb of your choice), finely chopped
175ml (6fl oz) tepid water
fine semolina powder, for rolling

- Begin by preparing the filling. Place a frying pan over a medium heat and, once hot, add the butter and onion. Cook, stirring occasionally, until very soft. This will take longer than you think – at least 15 minutes. If the onion starts to look a little dry, simply add a splash of water and turn down the heat. Add the vinegar and sugar and cook for a couple of minutes more, then set aside to cool completely.

- To make the dough, mix together the flour, salt, yeast, rosemary, cooled onions and water. Bring into a ball, then knead on a floured worktop until smooth and elastic. Cover with clingfilm (plastic wrap) and leave to rise until doubled in size – this should take an hour, depending on the temperature of your kitchen.

- Dust two baking sheets and your worktop liberally with the semolina. Gently tip the risen dough out on to the worktop, using a dough scraper to help you remove it from the bowl, then cut it in half using a sharp knife or dough scraper to form two rough triangles.

- Take one triangle and cut a line in the middle from 2cm (¾in) below the top to 2cm (¾in) above the flat edge. You are cutting right through the depth of the dough, but not right to each end, because you do not want to cut it completely in half. This line will be like a centre vein on a leaf. Now, on either side of that line, at a 45-degree angle, cut three little 'veins' in the same way. Stretch the dough so the holes open up. Repeat with the other piece of dough, then transfer to the baking sheets. Allow to prove until swollen and wobbly – again, this could take anything from 45 minutes up.

- Preheat the oven to 230°C/210°C fan/450°F/gas mark 8). Place two baking sheets or pizza stones in the oven to heat up. Slide the breads off their baking sheets (which should be easy if there's plenty of semolina beneath them) directly on to the hot sheets in the oven, spraying a mist of water inside before you shut the door. Bake for 12–15 minutes, or until golden brown and crispy. Cool slightly, then serve with salty butter.

7.

The Strictly Blessing

Performance is in my blood. Ever since I played the Magic Mirror in Chorley Little Theatre's adaptation of *Snow White*, back in 1993, I've longed for the stage. Naturally, I love an audience (Mum enjoys telling the tale of how I thrust myself out of my chair in the middle of a nursery school singing session, shouting, 'Let me sing on my own. Let me sing on my own!'), but there's something more sacred to performance than the resounding applause of an audience: separation. When you embody a character, of course you convey the superficial aspects of how they move their arms and where their 'centre' of energy is, but to get to that execution, you first have to consider the motive; the reasons why characters hold themselves a certain way. It's an unofficial study in psychology. And I love that. It allows you the opportunity to draw on the people you've met in your life, to consider their reasoning and background, and how their experiences have affected them physically.

It's that character portrayal that acts as a veil, a safety net between the audience's adoration and yourself. You can pat yourself on the back for doing a sterling job as an actor, but you know the intense emotion the audience feels emanates from the portrayal and not the self. It's that sense of grounding that makes the best actors of past and present. They have a passion, but it is a job, and it doesn't define who they are in every single recess of their lives.

That's true of the dance world, too. From about the age of twelve, I had dance lessons: modern, ballet, sometimes jazz. And if ever I performed as myself, I was a nervous wreck. I had to invent a character so that any missiles the audience fired off – of adoration or disappointment – weren't directed at me.

Beyond the limelight, of course, there's the company, and that is what I think I love the most. Back then, it was an opportunity to leave the boundless loneliness of the farm and integrate with my girlfriends. I felt accepted. I could be camp; I could be the true version of John. It was a stark contrast to the times relatives would tell me to not be 'too gay' at family parties when I danced to Destiny's Child. I don't think they were uncomfortable with me; I just think were they trying to protect me from the enquiring glances of others – glances that could easily have escalated into violence. But you don't consider motive when someone suppresses you. You just feel the bitter pain of the suppression itself, and without an understanding of the motive, you internalise the pain.

When Mum picked me up from dance lessons, we'd call in to the petrol filling station, where I'd get a brownie (the M&Ms

one with mini candies scattered on top) and a copy of the uber-masculine *FHM* magazine. What I really wanted to do was to lust over the men's underwear section of the Next catalogue, but I'd already spent my 'gay vouchers' at dance, and had to earn more by being a bloke. The freedom that dancing gave me – that sense of floating in the muscular clouds with angels – was bracketed, painfully, by the numbing dullness of the need to be something I was not.

After college, I didn't dance again. Even at parties with friends, I'd have to be blind drunk to allow myself to thrash around the dance floor. Just before the pandemic hit, Paul and I had begun going to Manchester more often, to the Gay Village, where I'd get mindlessly pissed and hurl my body around until the early hours. But rather than dancing in the clouds, this time it was in an underworld, in the dark depths of nightclubs, my movements fuelled by excessive amounts of booze. Not that there's anything wrong with nightclubs, but my reliance on them was becoming a point of concern.

Something inside me was burning to get out.

★ ★ ★

During the COVID pandemic, I was offered a role on *Steph's Packed Lunch*. I had been adamant that I wouldn't work in television again, but when my agent offered me a meeting with Steph and the team, I couldn't refuse. She was a powerhouse of a woman, yet always seemed so down to earth in her role as business correspondent on BBC news. When I first started working with her, she intimidated the crap out of me – that blend of intelligent quick wit and northern warmth can be disarming. But once we'd worked together for a while and saw each other as human and I realised she could take as much as she gave, I was grateful to have a twice-a-week slot on the soon-to-be Bafta-nominated TV show.

I certainly had fun while honing my skills as a television cook and presenter. If I wasn't swimming with sharks or making penises out of clay (by accident) on a pottery wheel, I was having my lunch cooked for me by Michelle Visage. The team welcomed me and pushed me to do more, to stretch myself and for me to believe in my own abilities.

At first, I started to exaggerate my personality and turn it all into a bit of a spectacle, making myself even more camp than I naturally was. I felt safe that way, because then I could be in on the joke too, like the gay presenters of the 90s. If we live up to a performative caricature of ourselves, we own the narrative. The editor, Vivek, and the food team, Sarah and Courtney, were kind. They reminded me that I didn't need to be anything other than myself. This was refreshing, because for years my management had struggled with the question 'who is John Whaite', and so I felt I needed to explain it with a limp wrist and a hand on my hip.

About seven months into that role, I got the call I'd secretly longed for since I won *Bake Off*. It was Easter weekend 2021, and I was painting the woodwork in the office at home. My agent rang me and asked, casually, 'What do you think about *Strictly*?'

My heart started to pound, but my brain soon kicked in, overriding the emotion with sense. I told him I liked it, loved it, longed to be on it, but knew that it was highly unlikely they'd want me. You hear stories of how even high-profile celebrities ask time and time again to be on the show, only to be refused until their moment eventually comes. Why would they want a part-time TV chef with far too much to say for himself? I wondered.

That's just my coping mechanism. After having experienced the knocks that every person in the industry inevitably suffers, you develop a coping strategy, a thick skin: until the contract is signed and you are filming the first episode, you have to tell yourself that it probably won't happen. But I proved my overly negative sense of 'realism' wrong when I found myself on a Zoom call with Stefania Aleksander and Sarah James, the talent and executive producers of *Strictly*. We chatted about life, dogs and performing. It was the kind of idle chit-chat you'd have with a work colleague – natural and unforced. Then they asked if I would be happy to be in the first all-male couple in the show's history, and my palms began to sweat. I wanted to say yes. I wanted to be boldly fearless and to represent my community, but the fear of being my default character of 'too gay' momentarily petrified my vocal cords. Perhaps I was hesitant, perhaps I wasn't – memory has a way of distorting time. All I know is that I said I would. In return, they promised they'd protect me from as much hate and bigotry as they could, just as my sisters, my lionesses, had done. And I instinctively trusted them. I was right to; they lived up to that promise.

Within weeks, I was in a dance studio in north London, pressed up against Giovanni Pernice, the Sicilian heart-throb of the show. They'd brought me down to dance for them, to see if I had an ounce of rhythm. Giovanni asked me what I wanted to learn, so we did a tango and a cha-cha. He was simply lovely: gentle and respectful of the fact I felt so deeply locked inside myself; he even gave me a little slap on the arse after we'd danced, which I found hilarious. The producers sat quietly in the corner, filming it on their iPhones to take back to the rest of the production company and to send to the BBC. They seemed to be impressed by my pace and learning capacity, and commented on how sweaty I had made Giovanni, saying he would never normally get so soaked during a dance test. I assumed they were just reeling off the usual showbiz bullshit, the small talk designed to make everything more comfortable. But a part of me felt that spark of performance that I hadn't felt for years. I felt a little bit more alive.

As I headed home on the train to Wigan, I cried. Partly from pride, partly from excitement, but also from a sense of sadness. Not just for myself, but for *all* the queer kids who'd grown up with a lack of representation on television. For the kids whose parents changed the channel if two men kissed in a soap opera. For the kids who saw gay storylines as outrageous and scandalous, rather than just another version of the desirable love stories we long to experience for ourselves. My hesitation, my need to be mindful of the potential flak and bigotry, said it all. Gay people have to wear blinders as we trot through life. We have to carefully select the bars we go into, the people we speak to, the clothes we wear. We watch as our brothers and sisters in other countries are hurled off buildings, beaten to death or shot in nightclubs. We sit and watch in agony, and think, 'There but for the grace of God go I.' This wasn't just a televised dance competition for me; this was a chance to make a small but mighty dent in the course of history. To make the queer kids of today feel seen, accepted, loved.

★ ★ ★

For months, I hounded my agent: 'Do they want me?', 'When will we hear from *Strictly*?'

Then, one glorious afternoon, he rang me and said excitedly, 'John, they're going to make you an offer. They're going to make you an offer tomorrow!' He was so proud of us, that we'd managed to get such an historic role on that show.

I was in the frozen-food aisle of my local supermarket at the time, probably reaching for a box of fish-fingers or a bag of petits pois. My body started to tingle with excitement and my ears started to ring – that stressful response that doesn't care whether the news is good or bad; it just consumes you physically. Paul looked at me and asked what was going on. I whispered the news to him over the soft-scoop. We drove home in silence. We both knew how mega it was to be booked on *Strictly*, but I think we both feared the toll it could take on our relationship. With the remnants of COVID still lurking, I wondered if I'd have to live in an isolated bubble, as the contestants of 2020 had. What would that mean for us?

Everyone I told was hugely excited: my parents, my sisters. My grandma was beside herself. None of them batted an eyelid when I said I was dancing with another man; they were proud. It was as though everything we'd been through as a family in relation to the bullying and their protection of me had led to this. It hadn't, of course, but I think it's only human: our default desire to interpret patterns as divine intervention.

The summer that year was one of languishing inactivity. *Steph's Packed Lunch* was off air for six weeks, and I had no other work on – my agent wanted to save my exposure for *Strictly* – so I sat, ruminating on everything. *What if the press digs into my sexuality? What if they have pictures of me falling out of nightclubs at 5am? What if they speak to people I've fallen out with and construct tales to bring me down?* The corrosive negativity of my own mind ate away at me. My agent did his best to reassure me, my therapist tried to get me seeing clearly, but nothing worked. I was manic and could barely sleep.

Towards the end of June, I injured my back in the gym, deadlifting improperly. I couldn't bend forward, and the pain shot down my left leg. I was bedbound for a couple of weeks and, apart from walking to appointments with my physiotherapist, I did not exercise. I started to severely reduce my calories for fear of putting on weight. In my mind, *Strictly* was partly about sex appeal, and I didn't want to undo the years of effort I had put into my fitness – particularly as the producers had given me the codename 'Hercules'. So I'd lie on the floor – the bed was too soft for my back – and watch shows about food to try and curb my cravings. I lived on diazepam and rice crackers spread with fish paste and sriracha. I didn't tell my agent or the producers about my injury, because I knew they'd make me delay my participation in the show; instead, I just told them I had a bit of backache and that it would clear up.

During that period of doing nothing, I worried. This time not about the press, but about the public's perception of a male–male partnership. Opinion had been mixed the year before when Olympic boxer Nicola Adams was paired with professional dancer Katya Jones. Was I ready to allow myself to be that vulnerable? What if I became a laughing stock and let my community down, serving only to fortify bigoted opinions about queer people? What if the LGBTQ+ kids saw me fail, and allowed that to percolate into their sense of self-worth?

I told my agent I wanted to be paired with a straight man – Kai or Graziano (for the height) – because homophobic people would accept that more. I started to bend my own values to pander to the abusers. I allowed the past – the bullying, the discomfort – to define my present and near future.

As I lay there, inactive and overthinking, I considered the bullies at high school. I felt the pain of loss for the people who had been prosecuted or severely persecuted – killed, even – just because of their sexuality. I looked at the life Paul and I had built over the past thirteen years together; we had flicked our 'fuck-it' switches, ignored the people who would rather have seen us living alone as hermits and devoted ourselves to one another. This wasn't *just* an opportunity for the LGBTQ+ children of today; it was an opportunity for us, too. It was also an opportunity to pay homage to the older generations of queer people who had rioted in the streets, paving the way for the liberties we now enjoyed. Or perhaps those people who had had to hide who they were for the majority of their life, forced to deny their own reality, even to themselves. It is for those people that we must scream the loudest. And while we must never take our eyes off the ball, we need to celebrate our victories for the same reason. To hide away, insist that I dance with a straight man, would be to deny my own rights – and, worse, those of others. I flicked my 'fuck-it' switch once more, and agreed to dance with a gay man – the beautiful South African, Johannes Radebe.

★ ★ ★

When Johannes dances, it is like nothing else exists in the world. He is a wild horse, running through the sand and dust, leaving everything behind in his wake. To dance with him was transcendent. I'd never felt supported like that, with such a graceful strength. To dance with another man seemed, in the moment, like everything I'd needed in my life. It was a contrast to when a gang of lads signed up to the dance group I was part of one Thursday night, just to mock me. Johannes felt the same. He often said how 'healing' our partnership was for him: for his family back home in the Free State, South Africa, to see his truth, his reality.

But with that shared experience comes dangerous territory. Compassion and empathy can easily metamorphose into something more powerful, more bonding. Johannes knew that could happen; he'd seen it a thousand times with his dance companions over the years. When you're physically pressed against another man for ten hours a day, things move emotionally. With that in mind, he was distant, pretty much from the start. I thought he hated me. He didn't, of course, and we've since become close friends. In the dance studio, we did what we had to do – we performed our dances and laughed together – but every lunchtime or break, he'd disappear. I can count on one hand the number of times we ate together.

In the evenings, I'd go back to the flat in Finchley, north London, that the production company had provided for me, Paul and Abel. I'd hit the red wine and whisky every night and binge on food. Most evenings, I'd raid the Little Waitrose across the road for Belgian buns, cornflakes and packet sandwiches, which I'd eat in a glossy-eyed frenzy, then force out of me. My bulimia got worse and worse as the weeks went on, and my relationship with Johannes became increasingly strained. It's not that we didn't get on; it's just that there was a firm boundary in place, and I didn't understand how someone could be so physically close to me, yet so detached. I wouldn't comprehend his perspective – his desire to guard his heart – until well after the competition had concluded.

Paul looked at me one day, as I stood red-faced and watery-eyed after throwing up, and told me, 'You don't have to do this, you know? You can drop out if it's causing you this much pain.'

But I couldn't drop out. I had to see this through, to the bitter end. All the times I'd failed or dropped out echoed in my mind, and I didn't want to be the ultimate disappointment to anyone. On screen, Johannes and I were bosom buddies, bonded and close. And that *was* real, it *felt* real. Of course, *Strictly* is like a political candidacy campaign. You have to garner votes. But you can tell when the couples are playing a game; they reel off the same bullshit spiel week after week, rehearsed – *Sickly Come Dancing*, more like. But I felt as though Jo and I were being honest – reactive, but honest. Emotions in the dance room were stifled, but seemed to come out as we danced – I was sure of that.

★ ★ ★

I rarely cooked during the thirteen weeks of the show. I just didn't have time. If we weren't eating Paul's turkey chilli, we were inhaling McDonald's or chips and gravy in the local pub – even though, when I ordered that particular combination, the waiter looked at me with nothing short of disgust – I don't think southerners will ever understand the joy chips and gravy can bring, but that's OK. I did bake a couple of times. My fellow contestant, Adam Peaty, asked if I made granola bars or flapjacks, so I rustled up a batch for him. I thought he might share them out, but I believe he and his dance partner, Katya, demolished the lot themselves. No wonder he has gold-medal stamina! I also made a batch of my salted caramel brownies for the production team and the lovely Liv Dias, who was the most brilliant television runner I have been fortunate enough to work with. Every morning, she'd steal a stash of jelly sweets from the green room and put them in my dressing room, then fill my fridge with cola and Red Bull, ready for the pre-show sugar boost I always needed. Nancy Xu, the professional dancer, made me a tiramisu one weekend and left that on the dressing-room coffee table. I inhaled the lot and couldn't get to sleep, thanks to the potent mixture of caffeine and post-show adrenaline. I told her about my gingerbread latte tiramisu, longed to make it for her, but sadly never found the time.

★ ★ ★

The sparkly side to *Strictly* was wonderful. I wouldn't say I was *most* excited about the free spray tans, but they were certainly a perk of the job. The tanning girls became such a vital connection to the real world – because of COVID, we were advised to limit contact with everyone, including the other dancing couples on the show, which didn't help neutralise the intensity of the competition. The girls and I would laugh about things in the news and tell jokes as I stood there in my skimpy thong while they doused me in Venetian Plus on a Friday night. They filled me in about a former celebrity contestant who had been told, by a *Strictly* alumnus, that you had to be completely naked for the spray tans. He'd marched into the tanning room, dropped his gown and bared all. I thanked God for my skimpy thong. After the tan, I'd head to the flat in the car, wrapped in my dressing gown, smelling of that soggy, oaty, digestive-biscuit aroma fake tan gives you, avoiding the paparazzi, who waited en masse at the gates.

Friday was always an exciting day, because we'd get to rehearse our dance on the ballroom floor three times. That's when it started to come together, and all the hard work seemed to pay off. It was exciting – except for the time Johannes kicked me in the head as we entered a lift during our Charleston. I almost passed out and had to take a breather. Earlier in the week, I'd knocked him in the mouth, busting his lip. It wasn't nearly as graceful as the polished version seen on a Saturday night. In rehearsals, knees get knocked and delicate parts get bruised.

It felt like so many of the production team were treading carefully to avoid risking the audience's acceptance of us. That belief was only fortified a year later, when journalists wrote hurtful things about the more gloriously camp pairing of Ritchie Anderson and Giovanni Pernice, comparing them to mine and Johannes' 'masculinity' – whatever that meant. It consolidated my belief that unless something is palatable and easy to watch and digest, it isn't wanted. So I have to emphasise just how bloody brave Stef and Sarah, the producers, were to set in motion such monumental change to the man-and-woman narrative of the show.

I knew they were protecting us, by the outfits they gave us to wear. While I'd envisioned myself topless, swathed in bedazzled mesh, or floating down the corridors of Elstree Studios with a train of toile behind me, it was all a little disappointingly sober. I'd often plead with Vicky Gill – the chief costume designer and one of the most gorgeous human beings I've ever met – to let me be a little more 'slutty', but she wanted to cover me up. During our rumba, I wore a sheer blue shirt, which I kept unbuttoning over the course of the dress rehearsal. Minutes before I went live on air for Saturday's performance, Jane, one of the sterner – but equally lovely – design team members, marched over and sewed my shirt shut. I was tempted to rip it off, to unpick the stiches with my teeth, to sod them all and just be extravagant and fabulous, but the words 'Don't be too gay' haunted me. Not just in terms of what I wore, but how I executed the dance moves. I wanted to be free, to dance with flair and abandon, but that voice held me back.

The dance team – the wonderful Jason Gilkinson, Ash-Leigh Hunter and Arduino Bertoncello – tried to get me to give a little more: 'That's good, but find the next level,' Jason would say. He could see I was holding back. *I* could see I was holding back; I could *feel* it. But I didn't know how to silence that voice.

Naturally, there was some external flak. We'd anticipated it, but it still hurt. People would message on Instagram saying how wrong it was to see two men dancing together. I'd expected that from men – I'd been conditioned to expect it – but when women said such things, they hurt more. I didn't think, for example, that a middle-aged mum of three could be so vociferously against our existence, but hate takes all forms. It's a shapeshifter. Worse, some fellow gay people complained to us. 'It should be about the dancing, not a Pride parade!' one harped.

We didn't want it to be about anything other than the dancing – of course we didn't. But dance is an expression of reality. It is art imitating life. My concerns were getting the steps right, but how could we not acknowledge the gravity of this huge change? The *first* male couple in the history of the show. We wanted it to be about equality; that's all we wanted. But equality is first preceded by justice, and justice and equality do not balance. Justice outweighs equality. It has to, because justice is the necessary antidote to injustice – prejudice. Justice paves the way for equality. It all takes time.

Johannes received some racist abuse, too. How he didn't crumble under the weight of that, I'll never know. It's one thing to be hated because you're gay; it's another to be hated because you are gay and Black. Some people would try to compensate and say things like 'I don't see race, I just see people', but that in itself is somewhat racist. To choose *not* to see a distinction, however noble the intention, is to choose to ignore the years of inequality people of colour have had to endure. It is to choose not to acknowledge that Black people are, at the time of writing, seven times more likely to be stopped and searched by the police than white people.

This wasn't just about dancing; this was about breaking down so many barriers. I couldn't give up. I couldn't let a childish feeling of not being adored by my companion, the lack of sexy outfits or the weight of unkind words force me to ruin it for myself. I had to grow up, flick that 'fuck-it' switch once more. I had to bite down on the bit and canter.

Just as heavy, in its own way, as the weight of the flak and social-media trolling, was the adoration of the fans. My inbox was filled with quite literally thousands of messages every single week. People loved our dancing and everything we stood for. And while that was hugely reassuring, it made me panic. *What happens when this is over?* I had already felt the painful comedown as time moved on after *Bake Off*. I knew I had to fortify myself against the ebb and flow of the industry in which I worked. Fans won't always be adoring. After each time we danced, I'd hang my costume on the rack in our dressing room and say, sometimes out loud, sometimes in my mind, 'Thank you for the fun, thank you for the thrill, but this all belongs to the dancefloor. This all belongs to *Strictly*.' I made sure I thanked every person I could before I left the studio each time – I wanted to remember, to never allow myself to forget in the tidal wave of adoring fans, that we were a company.

Our partnership had deeply affected both Johannes and me. It had freed us from the fetters we'd grown up with. As we walked on to the dancefloor for the last time, as the people behind the scenes clapped for us as the final VT rolled, Johannes began to cry. We got into position, raised our heads to one another, and I saw tears streaming down his face, glistening in the spotlight.

There it was.

There *he* was.

I felt things for him.

I repeated the words I'd told him every single time we waited in the wings to take the floor: 'It's just you and me.' I kissed the back of his hand, as I always did, and he kissed the back of mine in return, as he always did. Then he broke the tension and told me, as he often did, to sort out my 'pee-pee' – one must flatten one's appendage upwards against the underwear, to avoid any distracting flopping while dancing. What a way to break the tension!

After that final dance, as I hung up my clothes for the last time, I felt a sense of loss. Not because the competition was over – I was knackered and ready for a break – but because I wouldn't get to see Johannes every single day. I watched him as he sat on the windowsill of the dressing room drinking a glass of champagne, still sparkling in his bright-white Showdance outfit. I was jealous of the sweat beads as they shimmered on his beautiful skin. I wanted to be close to him. I felt mad at him for rushing away, for not staying for more than one drink. After *all* we'd been through. But he had to catch a flight to South Africa for Christmas, and he didn't want to risk cosying up at a party where COVID might have been rife. We hugged goodbye. I didn't want to let go.

'*We* did that!' he told me.

'*We* did that!' I replied.

We did that, indeed.

I realised as I stood there after our dance, clutching Johannes as he cried on my shoulder, that *I* – John, the farmer's son from Wigan, the 'fat fucking faggot' from high school, the one who dances a little 'too gay' at family weddings – had done that. It wasn't a character'; it was me. I don't know when that sense of self had kicked in. Maybe it had been there all along? Maybe even the moments when I had doubted myself and feared letting myself go were all part of some divine plan? But by the end of the show, I no longer felt as though I was portraying a character. It was just me, raw and true. In the moment, I had no cares left to give about what any single person in the world thought of me.

And that was a blessing – the *Strictly* blessing.

★ ★ ★

When we started the five-week-long *Strictly* tour, our friendship was stronger than ever. The stress of the competition, of the television performance, had melted away. We were now just repeating our two dances, night after night. We'd drink double JD and Cokes – Johannes' tipple of choice – and go shopping together. We'd eat lunch and dinner together. We'd sit together on the coach, laughing, chatting, being stupid. The guard had dropped, and we became inseparable. I learned he had kept his distance out of respect: to Paul, to me, to himself. I wish I had known, because I'd have been immediately able to empathise with that. It taught me a great deal about myself – I assume the worst. If only I had just considered that he was being cautious, in a world where millions of eyes were on us.

Strictly has a magical way of revealing the truth – the importance of friends. Some came round regularly with dinners to keep me fuelled, so I didn't have to worry about cooking, though Paul, my darling Paul, kept food in the fridge at all times. Some messaged me daily to make sure I was OK, to check in, to ask how it was all going. Some sent care parcels from home, with Lancashire cheese and pork pies, whisky and sleeping pills. It makes you realise the important things in life are those right next to us: the people we love.

I realise how much I missed Dad, and how connected we both had been to the arts. How it was something I inherited from him. As he sat in the audience for our paso doble to *Pirates of the Caribbean*, I didn't feel the same anxiety I had felt when Mum was there the week before. Now I just felt relaxed and unafraid. It didn't matter if I messed up and was voted off the show.

While I was sad that I didn't really get to make new strong friendships during the show – they had to keep us all separate because of the risk posed by the pandemic – we certainly made up for it on the live tour. Sara Davies, Maisie Smith, Tilly Ramsay and I became a little foursome and were inseparable for the duration. We'd sneak, like schoolkids on a residential trip, into each other's rooms and order wine and mixers from room service. We'd get bottles of gin and tequila and get trolleyed, laughing and joking all night – sometimes until 4am, the night before a two-show day. One night, Sara, the big sister of the group, had to put me to bed. She took my clothes off and I looked down, mortified. I was wearing a new thong that was a little on the small side, and my left testicle was poking out. We all stood there, me with one bollock hanging out, howling with laughter.

The television show had been sort of hard work – I say 'sort of', because compared to working two jobs to feed your children and pay the mortgage, it was a walk in the park, but it wasn't without its intense pressure. I was so engrossed in it all – the sparkle, the competition, the distraction from real life – that I never witnessed to the change in seasons. I started *Strictly* at the sweltering height of summer and left when morning frost blanketed the ground, but I didn't see that magical transition period that I usually love. I ignored the autumn.

The schedule had been exhausting. The tour, however, was something different: a five-week-long party with a little bit of work every night. When it all came to a close – the whole *Strictly* experience – I felt that same pang of emptiness I had felt after *Bake Off*. I started revisiting destructive habits, like going out drinking and staying out all night in Manchester, catching the first train home in the morning.

The mundane, with which I'd grounded myself in Canada and achieved a sense of security and peace, seemed to be the thing that irked me most now, and I didn't want to go back to normal life. I knew I had to, but it was so hard to say goodbye to it all, to everyone. For a while, Paul and I had to have some time apart. I felt like I didn't know what I wanted from my existence any more.

He told me, 'You need to figure out the man you want to be, what your values are, and how to live by that.'

He was forgiving and understanding of my situation – that my heart was torn in two – but, most impressively, he put himself first during the whole thing. He, of course, wanted to make sure I was OK – and he did – but he refused to let his own life be eroded by the aftermath of it all; he refused to be an anchor left to rust at the bottom of the ocean after the ship sailed away . He had the most beautiful and gracious strength and sense of self. While I sat on the patio, drinking bottle after bottle of Sauvignon Blanc, he reconnected with friends, went for walks with his family. There was nothing he could do for me while I was lost in this fog.

It was as though I was having an out-of-body experience the entire time. I knew I was being destructive – not just to my relationship, but also to myself. One afternoon, I drove into Manchester to get a gift for a friend's birthday. I planned to nip in, get the gift and go home. I woke up the next morning in my car, half a kebab by my feet. Thank goodness sleeping was all I had done in there. I don't even remember how I'd got into such a state. I'd met a friend for a beer, and one beer must have turned into a total bender. Months before, I had made history on the dancefloor, covered in sequins, not a hair out of place. I had filled children with pride and hope for their own future. I had helped people see past the paradigm of 'man and woman'. And now, here I was, in last night's clothes, stinking of alcohol, hair dishevelled and chilli sauce all over my shoes. The contrast was stark, and I was deeply ashamed of myself.

The glitterball and sequins may have reflected the tits and the teeth and the limelight to the audience, but I was now trapped inside a spherical hall of mirrors, confronting myself.

On my birthday, I sat alone with a McDonald's chicken burger. Paul had moved back in with his parents, and had taken Abel with him. I thought to myself, *What the hell are you doing?* I was making that childhood premonition of growing old alone come true. I was allowing my behaviour – the things I was trying so desperately to run away from – to destroy the beautiful life I had been running towards. Fourteen years in a solid relationship with a man who loved me unconditionally, a man who would move the Earth to make me feel safe, and I was pissing all over it. On the outside, I was winning awards with Johannes for our ground-breaking performance: the LGBT award and the Attitude award I had been hoping to win since I had been a fluffy-haired fledgling in the industry some ten years before. But none of that mattered. I was already proud of my achievements on screen, and as lovely as those awards were, as much as the younger me had lusted after them, what mattered now was fixing my real life and showing up for the man I loved – the man with whom I had fantasised about winning such awards and who should have been there by my side.

Peachy Peaty's Granola Bars

––––––

MAKES 12

During *Strictly*, Adam 'Peachy' Peaty asked me to make him some granola bars, and this was the precise recipe I used. He loved them so much that he and his dance partner, Katya Jones, ate them all to themselves. I didn't hold it against him – he's such a beautiful human.

70g (2½oz) unsalted butter, plus extra for greasing
225g (8oz) jumbo rolled oats
50g (1¾oz) desiccated (dried shredded) coconut
50g (1¾oz) pumpkin seeds
65g (2¼oz) dried sour cherries or cranberries
½ teaspoon ground nutmeg
115g (4oz) agave syrup, golden syrup or honey
50g (1¾oz) light brown muscovado sugar
zest of 1 small orange
½ teaspoon fine salt

- Preheat the oven to 200°C/180°C fan/400°F/gas mark 6. Grease a 20cm (8in) square cake tin and line with baking paper (parchment paper).

- Scatter the oats, coconut and pumpkin seeds on to a baking sheet and toast in the preheated oven for 10–15 minutes, or until lightly golden. Allow to cool, then pour into a large mixing bowl and add the cherries or cranberries and nutmeg. Toss together.

- Reduce the oven temperature to 170°C/150°C fan/340°F/gas mark 3½.

- Put the syrup, butter, sugar, orange zest and salt into a saucepan and set over a medium–high heat. Allow everything to melt together. Pour the melted mixture into the mixing bowl and stir well, ensuring everything is completely coated.

- Tip the mixture into the prepared cake tin and press down well to compact. Bake for 25–30 minutes, or until lightly golden. Remove from the oven and allow to cool completely, before slicing into 12 rectangles.

- These will keep for 5 days stored in an airtight container.

Gingerbread Latte Tiramisu

———

SERVES 6–8

After the lovely Nancy Xu made me one of the best tiramisus I'd ever had during my time on *Strictly*, I told her about this recipe. I never managed to find the time to make it, so instead I'll dedicate it to her. It's a riff on the winter coffee-shop classic, the gingerbread latte, but in tiramisu form. I've swapped the traditional savoiardi biscuits for sticky ginger cake, and the result is divine.

butter, for greasing
2 large eggs, whites and yolks separated
50g (1¾oz) caster (superfine) sugar
100ml (3½fl oz) marsala wine (or sweet sherry)
100ml (3½fl oz) Kahlua
250g (9oz) mascarpone cheese
250g (9oz) double (heavy) cream
1 tablespoon instant coffee dissolved in 1 tablespoon hot water
2 readymade ginger loaf cakes, like McVitie's Jamaica Ginger Cakes, cut into 1cm (½in) slices
100g (3½oz) dark chocolate, very finely chopped (I do this in a mini food processor)

- Grease a deep 20cm (8in) square cake tin and line with baking paper (parchment paper).

- Put the egg whites into a freestanding electric mixer fitted with a whisk attachment (or you can do this with a handheld electric whisk if you prefer). Whisk the whites to stiff peaks, then pour in the sugar, whisking all the while, to form a stiff meringue.

- Scoop the meringue into a separate bowl, then, into the mixer bowl (there's no need to clean it) add the yolks, 2 tablespoons each of marsala and Kahlua, and the mascarpone. Whisk to combine, then add the cream and whisk just until soft, floppy peaks form – this will take about 3 minutes. The mixture must not be too stiff, or the finished tiramisu will be dry. The cream should hold its shape very reluctantly.

- Add a third of the egg whites to the cream mixture and fold in, then add the rest and fold in until completely smooth – this is best done with a balloon whisk or flat spatula.

- In a small bowl, mix the rest of the marsala and Kahlua with the coffee.

- Line the base of the prepared cake tin with a layer of ginger cake slices and soak them well with the alcohol-and-coffee mixture. Top with half of the mascarpone mixture, then scatter on half of the chocolate. Repeat with another layer of cake, soak as before, then top with the remaining mascarpone and finish with the remaining chocolate.

- Leave to set in the fridge, preferably overnight, before serving.

Millionaire's Brownies

———

MAKES 16

I can't remember what week of *Strictly* it was when I made a
batch of brownies, but I remember sharing them out at the dance
studio among some of the couples. We couldn't spend much time
together or even near one another because of COVID, but that
certainly didn't stop me from sharing my bakes. These brownies,
with a layer of salted toffee, topped with a thin crust of dark
chocolate, sprinkled with sea salt went down particularly well
with everyone – why wouldn't they?

For the brownies
200g (7oz) dark chocolate (50–60 per cent cocoa solids),
roughly chopped
200g (7oz) unsalted butter, cubed, plus extra for greasing
265g (9½oz) caster (superfine) sugar
130g (4¾oz) plain (all-purpose) flour
20g (¾oz) cocoa powder
½ teaspoon fine salt
3 large eggs

For the caramel layer
397g (14oz) can condensed milk

150g (5½oz) light brown muscovado sugar
100g (3½oz) unsalted butter
40g (1½oz) golden syrup
2 teaspoons vanilla bean paste
½ teaspoon fine salt

For the chocolate layer
200g (7oz) dark chocolate (50–60 per cent cocoa solids),
roughly chopped
20g (¾oz) sunflower oil
sea salt flakes

- Preheat the oven to 180°C/160°C fan/350°F/gas mark 4. Grease a 20cm (8in) square cake tin and line with baking paper (parchment paper), folding the excess paper over the sides of the tin and securing in place with small bulldog clips.

- For the brownie batter, put the chocolate and butter into a heatproof bowl and set over a pan of barely simmering water. Stir occasionally, allowing the chocolate and butter to melt together. Remove the bowl from the heat and stir in the sugar, followed by the flour, cocoa powder and salt, then beat in the eggs. The mixture will go a little grainy and may split when the eggs are first added, but keep beating and it will come together into a smooth and glossy batter. Pour the batter into the prepared tin and bake for 30 minutes, or until the top is matte and cracked around the edges. Allow to cool completely.

- To make the toffee layer, put all the ingredients into a saucepan and set over a low heat until everything melts together and the sugar has dissolved. Increase the heat to medium–high and allow the mixture to boil. Stir frequently until it reaches 105°C (221°F) on an instant-read digital thermometer – there may be a few dark flecks, but that's perfectly fine. Pour the cooked toffee over the cooled brownie layer, then refrigerate for a few hours until very firm.

- Once the toffee layer has set, put the chocolate and oil into a heatproof bowl and set over a pan of barely simmering water. Allow the chocolate and oil to melt together, then pour over the cold toffee layer and quickly top with a sprinkling of sea salt. Refrigerate for another hour before cutting into 16 squares to serve. These are best stored in the fridge in an airtight container, where'll they keep for a week.

8.
The Man with Sore Feet

———

After the glitter of the whole *Strictly Come Dancing* experience had settled, and as Paul and I tried to figure out what our future, if we had one, looked like, I needed to get away. I wanted a break from everything, a chance to collect my thoughts. I had countless meetings with people from different industries: merchandise, production companies, channel commissioners, Andrew Lloyd Webber's West End theatre production company. Day after day, there was something new and exciting, but it rarely came to anything. I felt spread thin, like the last nugget of butter, eked too far across multiple slices of toast. What I needed wasn't an indulgent all-inclusive holiday with pissed-up strangers promising to become lifelong friends, but a challenge.

I was knackered – mentally and physically exhausted – but I needed a physical struggle away from the razzle-dazzle of showbusiness, one that would allow me to recalibrate and reassess my values. A moment to digest what the bloody hell had happened over the past year or so. I felt as if I had been in one of those Japanese game shows – *Takeshi's Castle* – running an assault course while pineapples and mud bombs were being hurled at me. It had been fun, and I had loved every minute, but my mind and my body had had enough.

On a train journey from London back to Wigan, I had a little too much whisky and decided I would do the West Highland Way in Scotland. A friend of mine had trekked the ninety-six miles a few years earlier with a group of friends. She'd taken her springer spaniel, Bracken – Abel's grandma – and over the course of a week or so, had walked, camped, existed. That's precisely what I wanted to do. By the time the two-or-so-hour train journey was over, I'd planned my entire route: the miles I would do each day (around twenty), the campsites I would stay in (I wasn't going to wild-camp and risk being slaughtered by some kilted, chainsaw-wielding forest-dweller). I'd ordered a one-man tent, along with most of the other equipment that various blogs recommended, and then I tumbled off the train, steaming drunk.

'But you don't really like walking!' was the first thing Paul said to me when I told him my plan.

I did like walking, and he knew that, but ever since I'd thrown a wobbler in Grizedale Forest on one of our earliest dates, the ghost of me not being a walker had haunted our relationship. It was an impulsive decision, I'll give him that, but I believe there are two versions of impulsivity in my character. One, the flawed side, drinks too much, spends too much on trinkets and tchotchkes, speaks before he thinks and sometimes says devastating things. The other is a survival mode, an instinctive impulsion, a visceral knowledge of what I need when I myself don't even know it – much like how the decision to flee to Canada was in fact me kicking my own feet away beneath me in order to stay afloat.

After the turbulence caused by *Strictly* to our relationship – the most treacherous we'd experienced so far – Paul was rightly concerned that this could be the conclusion to us. He was worried he could lose me for ever – just as I had been worried about losing him when the aftermath of *Strictly* plunged me into a deep, thick head fog. He knew he had to give me the space to decompress and process it all, but he was scared.

As we parted on the pathway out of Milngavie – the starting point of the walk – he told me he'd put a notepad in my rucksack, and he wanted me to read what he had written in there when I set up camp on the first night. I was itching to rip open the bag the moment he and Abel trotted out of sight, but I wanted to be patient and to respect his instructions. I turned to look back, grains of sand on the horizon representing my entire world, and I just knew that I wasn't walking away from them, from us – I was walking home. I was trekking to repair the damage that I had caused with my emotional destruction. I knew he'd be there at the finish line in Fort William, nearly one hundred miles ahead of me, and that I would run to him, fall into his arms, kiss him passionately, like lovers reunited after the painful distance of war. Drama queen.

* * *

The first half of the first day was a relatively easy hike. Most of it was haunted by the murmur of the A81: a noise that serves as a constant reminder of civilisation; which in itself delivers thoughts of relationships concomitant with their ups and downs; of industry and the hierarchy; of it being about not what you know but who you know. I looked at the mountaintops in the distance and thought to myself, *Does God really give a shit about profit margins and GDP?* Even the sheep, as they nonchalantly grazed in the fields, seemed desensitised: 'Oh look, Eunice, there goes another lost soul on a spiritual quest!'

The walk is easy to navigate. Signposted by wooden markers etched with a thistle inside a hexagon, you would really struggle to lose your way. Those markers, combined with my guidebook, meant that I knew precisely where I was going. Pathways became country lanes, which became wooden walkways through marshlands, which became old railway paths of gravel and dust.

I looked up at the bright-blue skies, then down at my grey walking boots – a very cheap pair that I'd bought because the expensive Meindl boots I'd spent an entire morning being expertly measured up for were simply too big and clunky, and made me look like the love child of Father Christmas and an adventure penguin. These grey ladies matched my leggings and rucksack perfectly – not that I'm a fashionista, but, being colour-blind, I mind about colours matching. Even as a child, I dreaded looking like a patchwork quilt.

But halfway into that first day, I regretted my mindless footwear choice. When I arrived at Drymen village, my feet were throbbing, and I raided the local chemist for Compeed plasters. Outside, a car slowed down, beeped its horn and the family inside it waved frantically at me, excited to see the lad from *Strictly*. I forgot my pain for a second, waved back, fulfilled my role.

I sat in the Drymen Inn and devoured a full English, a mug of coffee and a pint-of-lager chaser, then heated a safety pin in the flame of a cigarette lighter and popped my blisters: one on every toe, each bigger than the digit it inhabited. I stuck layers of plasters on to my feet, bound my toes with duct tape (never go on a camping hike without a roll of duct tape) and hobbled the final ten miles or so. Each step was accompanied by a 'bastard!' or a 'fuck my life!'. The scenery here on the edge of the Highlands was breathtaking, but I had no breath left to take after my foul-mouthed exhalations. The moment I saw the glisten of Loch Lomond peeking through the pine trees of Garadhban Forest, I imagined hurling my cheap boots skyward and bathing my throbbing feet in the cold, healing water. For a moment, I smiled, calmed by the image, but as so often with oases, the illusion faded, and my steps were once again partnered with pain and profanity.

As I traipsed the final couple of miles or so, cars seemed to slow to inspect this weary-looking figure hobbling along the footpath. I was tempted to stick out a thumb, to hitch a ride and cheat, but then something I'd recently read came rushing back to me. *I May Be Wrong* by Björn Natthiko Lindeblad is a gentle memoir of a former financier-turned-forest monk. In one part, he describes how he was returning to a monastery after a long pilgrimage, when a man on a motorbike offered him a lift. Björn told the man he must complete the mission entirely on foot, and when the man said, 'No one will know,' Björn simply replied, 'I will know.'

Integrity is a fucker, I thought to myself, and hobbled on.

When I finally arrived at Milarrochy Bay campsite, I was ushered to a pitch on the edge of the loch, where I battled with the wind blowing across the water as I put up my tent. I boiled up some water for a hot chocolate and rehydrated beef chilli. I sipped the hot chocolate, its well-earned sweetness making me feel instantly reinvigorated, and opened my rucksack to retrieve Paul's notepad. He'd painstakingly filled page after page, listing all the values he saw in me, which perhaps I didn't see in myself. He told me that I didn't have any self-esteem, and listed the reasons why I should find it. *Yeah right*, I thought. I'd almost broken our relationship. I'd floated on the waves of audience applause for the past four months. I risked fourteen years of security and feeling safe, simply because my mind was a mess. I didn't think of myself as lacking in self-esteem; I saw myself as a spoilt, self-indulgent arsehole.

I sobbed. Sitting on a rock outside my one-man bivvy in between an inflatable colosseum of a tent filled with about twelve friends and a smaller tent with a young family, I stifled my gulps for air with my fleece, as Johannes had done with his towel when his lungs had stung after our dances. I was exhausted and my feet hurt, but this book of kindness from the only person I had ever felt certain about in my entire life was what brought me to my knees.

I looked at the lake, which was now eerily still, with the mountains reflected in its water. If I stood on my head, I wouldn't know which way was up or down. *Maybe,* I thought to myself, *there is no such thing as upside down.* Maybe the collateral beauty of any breakdown or momentary lapse in emotional wellbeing is that it offers a newfound perspective on it all. Maybe, as Mum had told me repeatedly in the past, we can't be happy every day. But does that necessarily mean misery or ugliness have to supersede everything? Perhaps misery doesn't exist; perhaps the opposite of happiness, of beauty, is simply upside-down happiness and beauty. Mum was right, you can't have happiness every day. That is sickly sweet. To be content should be enough.

What was in that hot chocolate?

I finished my chilli, dried my eyes, then peeled my feet out of my shoes. I thought about the first time I had lost my shoes from being drunk. Little black lace-ups with a squared-off toe. I was eight years old. Mum and my stepdad had gone to a New Year's Eve party, so my sister Victoria and I were left with all the other kids and teenagers at someone's house. I mine-swept the place, downing dregs from bottles of Hooch and Bavarian lager. I remember sitting cross-legged on the couch, swaying, as one older lad pointed and laughed. 'He's absolutely ratted.'

The next thing I knew, I was in my mother's arms, being sick over her shoulder and down her back. The morning after, I woke up fully clothed in my bed and wondered where my shoes were.

They were my school shoes, and I panicked I'd need them in a few days' time. I'd left them at the party.

* * *

When I woke up in my tent beside the loch the next morning, after a sleep disturbed by the howling wind and my throbbing feet, I couldn't walk. The pain was so severe that even in flip-flops, I could barely hobble at a snail's pace to the toilet. When I slipped my feet back into the walking boots of hell, I wanted to throw them beneath the wheels of an articulated lorry, and for it to reverse repeatedly over them until every atom of them was dispersed into the atmosphere and invisible to the naked eye. The pain burned in my toes. I had to get a taxi back to Glasgow, where I met Paul, who clutched the oversized Meindls with a knowing look in his eyes. The moment I stepped into them, the pain was gone. Why hadn't I just listened to John, the owner of Whalley Warm and Dry and all-round shoe expert, when he'd explained, in vast detail, why I needed that shoe in particular? I ended up having to spend that day in Glasgow with Paul – it was too late to set off walking again, and I didn't want to walk just a few miles. I wanted to reach my daily count, even if that meant setting off a day later.

First thing the next morning, Paul dropped me off at the lochside and kissed me goodbye for the second time on this vast adventure. Oh, the drama! He sped away in our orange car – our tangerine dream – and I carried on walking with the misty loch to my left. Herons perched on rocks in the still water, bearing witness as the carabiners on my bottles jangled with every pain-free step I took. I didn't care that these giant boots gave me the foot-to-height ratio of a moorhen. I was just so grateful that I could continue.

★ ★ ★

As the footpath abandoned the familiar friendliness of the loch, it ventured into dense woodland with a floor of moss greener than any I had ever seen – it was almost acid green. I chuckled as I remembered my stepdad forcing me to mow the lawn. I'd always wake up to a list of chores every Saturday, which I had to complete before I could watch *SMTV Live*. For the most part, it was things such as emptying or stacking the dishwasher and vacuuming the stairs, which I'd merrily do, grateful for an empty house in which I could lounge for the rest of the day. But in summertime, I'd wake up to the rattling wheels of the lawnmower being dragged across the gravel drive, and I'd know what lay in store.

'It's because I'm gay!' I'd eventually shout, after I had come out.

'It's not because you're gay,' my parents would reply. 'It's because you can't live here without contributing.'

The whole world, for a short time after I found the courage to admit my sexuality, seemed to revolve around me being gay. And anything that inconvenienced me was a homophobic slight. Even asking me to nip to the shops for some carrots was offensive.

As the pathway rose up into what seemed like an endless wood-and-soil staircase, I tightened my rucksack straps and started upwards. Two fell runners ran past me with ease, and I felt a green envy for their spritely lunges, unencumbered by a twelve-or-so kilogram rucksack.

I chuckled to myself as I remembered climbing Jack's Rake

in the Lake District with Paul, my cousin Tom and my sister Victoria. Tom, Victoria and I had carried proper day bags, discreet and unobtrusive, filled with water and carbohydrates. Paul had his Ally Capellino waxed-cotton satchel on his back, bulky and uncomfortable, not intended for such a strenuous scramble. We laughed as my cousin, sixteen stone (probably more) of pure muscle, quickly ascended the rockface like a mountain goat, while Paul fumbled up the ravine like a grizzly bear. He was remarkably cute, for such a broad-shouldered beast.

I started to crave cheese and apple: a crisp Granny Smith, sour and fresh, and a big block of creamy Lancashire cheese from Chorley market. That's what Victoria and I used to eat when we were kids – that, and sachets of Batcherlors Pasta 'n' Sauce, filled with glucose and other junk. I'd sit on the couch watching *Sleeping Beauty* (again!) and Our Vic would bring bowlfuls of apple and cheese, both perfectly diced to exactly the same specifications. We'd squeeze the cheese and warm it slightly in our fingertips, then stick it to a chunk of apple and nibble – my first experience of food pairing.

* * *

We've always been close, Our Vic and me. When we were small, way before our parents split up, we'd create little Christmas plays and act them out by the Christmas tree. In summer, when Dad cut the legs from his denim jeans to make shorts, Our Vic and I would each shove both of our legs into a single leg of his cut-off denim and thrash around the paddling pool pretending to be mermaids. When I was fourteen, it was with Our Vic that I tried my first line of cocaine. We were at a house party at some friends' place and a guy passed me a CD with a line of white powder on it and told me to snort it into one nostril with a rolled-up tenner. I did. It stung my nostril, tasted like bleach and left an awful mucus lump at the back of my throat and base of my nose. It was vile, but within a short while, I started to feel electric and untouchable. I was making everybody laugh, and I was confident and alive. It was a version of me that I had never met before.

Over the next few days of my hike, as the pathway returned to the loch, then veered away again for a final time, splitting into two, sometimes three, I consulted my guidebook and followed the markers. I put one foot in front of the other as I traversed the boundlessness of Rannoch Moor and tried to forget the route behind me, focusing solely on the route ahead.

It occurred to me that Our Vic and I had started on the same path. We'd walked the same dusty road as each other, but I had been given a destination: university. It wasn't necessarily a destination I had wanted, but the signposts of my journey seemed to point that way. For Our Vic, just as intelligent but not academic, the future was more of a mystery. She'd started hairdressing – and was bloody good at it, even opening her own salon with the help of our parents – but her journey seemed to be covered by clouds of confusion the entire time, while for me, the sun shone down. She walked the same pathway as I did, but she never got to change her shoes. She hobbled along in pain, and none of us knew until it was almost too late.

After a close friend of our family – best friend to Our Vic – was murdered, Vic seemed to spiral. But it was a spiral along a horizontal path, almost like a roller coaster. It wasn't a dramatic drop into inertia, but rather a decade-long battle of ups and downs. She seemed to be drinking more, losing things on nights out, not coming home for a day or two. I told my mum and Jane about the time I'd taken cocaine when I was fourteen, as I was worried Vic might have developed a habit, but they just got angry – aggressive, almost. There were glimmers of hope when she had her children, found a routine and things seemed to improve, but eventually I think the stress of child rearing, coupled with the pain she'd experienced, caught up with her, and her benders became more frequent, more dangerous. Sometimes, she'd flee the house in the dead of night, leaving her boys and her partner to wake up and find she was missing. We'd scour the village and text everyone who knew her to try and get her to come home.

On a holiday to Portugal, the same thing happened – she fled – and her then-fiancé had to fly home with her children. It was as though time stood still. No one knew where she was. I put a tweet out, begging for information. Vic had recently been diagnosed with pre-menstrual dysphoric disorder (PMDD). We hoped this was the explanation for her behaviour, and that treating it might offer a cure for these outbursts, but addiction had already taken hold of her by then.

I would have turned the earth barren just to find her, like

Persephone's mother. I remember my jaw shaking as I tried to get the words out: 'If she dies, and I haven't done everything I can to help her, I will kill myself.' I knew I would. I knew that, for too long, we hadn't done enough as a family. We'd been angry with her. We were the fallen trees looming over her on the bank of the River Styx, as she gasped for air and tried to stay afloat. We should have been her lifeboats.

It was difficult, because when addicts are in the midst of a binge, it's as though they're possessed by a demon. Speaking in tongues, they say hurtful things – some truths, some fallacies – and it takes a thick skin to be impervious to that. My family, all of us too emotionally dysregulated, had let those words fuel our fire and push us away. As a result, Dad and I exchanged some hurtful words as we reacted from our pain. We wouldn't speak for a year after that. Little pebbles left to roll became boulders that flattened the ground between us. We were still a family, but we were a jigsaw with the interlocking parts torn off.

I rang the British Embassy and the airport police, who were both unable to help. It reminded me of months before, when I'd accompanied Vic to hospital in an ambulance, and she'd been dismissed as yet another addict.

'She's just an alcoholic,' the mental health nurse had said to me.

What the hell did she mean by 'just'? I thought. Like a farmer justifying tying up his mutt in a snow-covered doghouse – it's *just* a dog. Like a fisherman bashing the brains out of a freshly captured river trout – it's *just* a fish. She wasn't *just* an alcoholic; she was my sister, and she was in pain. I wanted to scream at the nurse, tell her how the government was to blame for allowing alcohol to be so bloody cheap, so easily accessible, so socially encouraged (enforced, even), but she and her two-toned bob had already shuffled away to her office.

Eventually, a lady in Portugal found Our Vic and locked her in the bathroom to prevent her from running away or harming herself. Jane and the father of Vic's children flew out to bring her home, and for a few days she lived with me. I took her phone and bank card from her. We tried everything we could. Mum even snapped Vic's iPhone in half one morning after a binge with just her bare hands. I've never seen a person burning with such a desperate and devastated fire. But it didn't work. Nothing would. Addiction had her in its claws; she knew how to get her fix.

★ ★ ★

I noticed, on my walk, that each day got a little easier, and that I got a little stronger physically. I focused less on the footsteps – just one foot in front of the other – and more on the scenery. I thought more about God. I've never been a religious person. I'd laugh in my Church of England assemblies when teachers recited the biblical threats of hellfire and brimstone. *Bullshit*, I'd always think. It all seemed too certain, too factual. Wasn't faith supposed to be based on hope and belief? Faith is something I've always had. Every night, I say the same prayer as I drift off to sleep:

> *Lord, keep us safe this night,*
> *secure from all our fears,*
> *may angels guard us while we sleep*

till morning light appears.

But I don't believe in God in any rigid and orthodox sense. An omnipotent, omniscient fella in the clouds may well be dramatic, but it's a premise too easily accepted by a society conditioned to expect and surrender to hierarchy. God, for me, is love. It is forgiveness. It is empathy. As Mum always used to say back in the chippy, God is about putting others before yourself, and there is something in that noble truth. But as that other deity, RuPaul, rightly declares: 'If you can't love yourself, how the hell you gonna love somebody else?' Those words used to make me shudder whenever I watched *RuPaul's Drag Race*. I thought it was just an excuse for self-indulgent arseholes to be, well, self-indulgent. But now, I think the opposite is true. There's nothing self-indulgent about self-love, because self-love is discipline.

As I climbed the Devil's Staircase and reached the summit, I looked back towards Kingshouse and Altnafeadh, which sat beneath dark, looming clouds. As the wind battered me and rattled against my waterproofs, something Paul had said during the post-*Strictly* fallout echoed in my mind: 'Hell is a life of short-lived highs.' I was dumbfounded by this wisdom. He was so right. Our Vic's drinking and drug abuse, my drinking binges, my quest for external validation and fulfilment – they were all short-lived, transient, superficial stopgaps in our lives. They were diversions and distractions from the painful pilgrimage we all have to make as we gain wisdom from our experiences.

I thought back to that time at Jack's Rake, when I watched

Our Vic, who was by this point a year or so clean and sober. She had a freshness to her, an untouchable wisdom that radiated from her. Once reactive and volatile, she was now calm and considered. Her high of choice was the peak of a mountain or a long and heavy gym session. She had managed to find a strength inside herself, a deep-rooted respect, that enabled her to kick booze and drugs completely. It had taken a while, many AA meetings, more relapses – but my God, she had done it. I asked her what drove her to find sobriety. She said she had somehow come to realise, deep down inside, as she lay in rehabilitation centres and hospital beds, that she did not deserve that life. She wanted better for herself. She wanted to love herself so that she could love her family, her children. And she got there. Through exercise, mountain-climbing, therapy, she dragged herself from the depths of hell, kicking and screaming, scratching at the eyes of the devil.

She did it. And she is the best mum you could imagine. She is a hero.

★ ★ ★

The final day of the walk was hard: a really tough climb out of Kinlochleven, followed by a repetitive mountain pathway to Fort William. Our Vic's face burned brightly in my mind. Thinking of her gave me the strength I needed to march forward on this final monotonous effort, punctuated by stone ruin after stone ruin. As I arrived in Fort William to complete the walk, a couple on a bench laughed at my ginormous boots. I looked down, glanced back to the couple and laughed along. The boots did look ridiculous, but they had carried me all this way. I would be forever grateful to these blocks of leather and rubber.

My hope of falling into Paul's arms at the finish line didn't come true. He had texted to say he set off late and was caught in traffic. It wasn't the romantic, black-and-white movie ending I had anticipated, but it was perfect, nonetheless. For too long, I had relied on Paul to pick up the pieces, to catch me when I fell. For too long, I had shirked personal responsibility and sailed along in the wake of his values and morality.

I plonked myself beside the bronze statue that now famously marks the end of the West Highland Way, aptly named *The Man with Sore Feet*. I nodded at him then had a little chuckle. I slipped off my boots and quietly patted myself on the back. *Well done, lad.* The bright lights of *Strictly Come Dancing* may have taken me away from myself for a time, but this hike in the jagged highlands, scraping the moody skies and feeling that bit closer to God, had brought me humbly hobbling back.

9.
The Elephant in the Room

———

It's probably a bad move to make huge life decisions while on holiday. In fact, it's pretty damn reckless, but influenced by the emboldening combination of sun, sea and wine, I have certainly made some questionable choices. Like, for example, the time I refused to come home from Madrid after teaching English to Spanish youths, quite simply because I'd fallen in love with somebody. That's the gist, and that's all you need to know.

But one holiday decision that I later came to regret was joining the subscription-based content-creator platform, OnlyFans. The sun, sea and wine were indeed partly to blame for this; I was in Nice in 2022 after the busiest year of my life, and, propelled by the breeze of liberation we all feel while on vacation, I decided to move some content from Instagram to OnlyFans. I guess I was still feeling a certain emptiness after *Strictly Come Dancing*, and it didn't help that my agent had dealt me some bad news as I was on the way to the airport. So, the yin and yang of pre-holiday blues and mid-holiday euphoria definitely made for a dangerously sharp contrast.

Let me give a little backstory here. During the COVID-19 lockdown, in August 2020, to be precise, I became seriously interested in weightlifting. I'd always exercised, but had never properly paid attention to nutrition: things like more calories in (rather than the restriction I was used to), a high level of protein intake, when to eat and how to eat. As I paid more attention to what and how I ate, I saw my body take the shape I'd longed for: bigger shoulders, stronger arms and a chunky old booty. For the first time in my life, I felt comfortable being bigger. I no longer wanted to shrink away from the world, but instead felt as though I deserved to take up the space I had been assigned by whichever controlling force or deity is out there.

As I got leaner, stronger, fitter and shapelier, people commented more. At first, I paid these comments no mind, brushed them all off as shallow compliments. Before I knew it, though, the feeling had taken over, and I was defining myself by my physique. I don't know whether some algorithm on social media meant that the pictures and videos I shared that focused more on my body gained more traction, or whether it was simply because as rapacious human beings, we naturally stop in our tracks as we scroll upon beefcakes and buttocks. Whatever it was, I was getting viewing figures on Instagram like I'd never seen before.

My rational self saw what was happening and cringed. I was becoming so seemingly self-obsessed on social media. A story about a Victoria sponge would be followed by one of me in tight Lycra gym leggings, and as my likes and interaction increased, my sense of pride dwindled slightly. I'd go so far as to say that if *I* followed me on Instagram, I'd think I was a complete egocentric arsehole. I knew that my output was becoming less about my talents and the years of graft behind them and more about external validation. Every time I posted in this way, I felt cheap – guilty, almost. But I couldn't stop myself. The fizz of a like or fleeting comment far outweighed any sense of what I wanted to be and how I wanted to act.

My bulimia was bad at this time, too. If I didn't stick to my rigid eating plan, which included turkey chilli every single night for dinner and a high-calorie smoothie each morning, I'd go off the rails and binge and purge. After a heavy lifting session, I'd spin around McDonald's Drive Thru two or three times, eating 1,500–2,000 calories. I'd get home riddled with guilt and force myself to throw it up, before hitting a generous glass of whisky and a couple of sleeping pills to calm my mind. Paul was concerned, naturally, so we decided together that I should take up therapy again.

I could see myself from the outside looking in and I was ashamed of the man I was becoming – someone so obsessed with his image that I'd plan everything around a gym session. If I thought I wouldn't be able to fit one in, I'd have a panic attack or snap at my agent or family. But despite my inner sense telling me to stop, to quit the gym and focus on work and family, I carried on, hellbent on perfection. I even set up an Instagram account dedicated to my bodybuilding experience. It started off as weightlifting tips and exercises, but soon descended into cheap 'thirst traps' – pictures of my body in provocative poses or from suggestive angles. I should add I worked hard for the body I had – fifty hours a month in the gym, sometimes – but was I truly taking care of myself? Absolutely not. My mum knew, as many mums do, when I was just exhausted. She'd almost beg me to go home and get into bed, but her words rang empty in my ears. I couldn't see the love for the ambition. The external validation was instantly gratifying and overrode what those who loved me were telling me.

Strictly Come Dancing had offered a kind of repose from this, because my social media became flooded with dance-related content. Naturally, people were lapping that up. With the hours I was putting in with Johannes in the dance studio, I didn't have time in the final few weeks of the competition to work out. I put on fat and lost muscle – something I had vowed would never happen to me – but I didn't seem to mind. At that time, I wasn't the same empty ghost seeking the approval of others as a reason to walk the earth. I was deeply proud of my progress in the competition and the work Johannes and I had put in, and that momentarily silenced the body dysmorphia. As I've already shared, I still had terrible episodes of bulimia during my time on *Strictly*, but they were, I think, more of a coping strategy due to the sense of being utterly out of control that came with being vulnerable on a dancefloor in front of ten million people each week. Even the most level-headed person would struggle with that, I think.

I had met a few friends over the years who had been very successful on OnlyFans. Kerry Katona, a colleague on *Steph's Packed Lunch*, had made a fortune through the site and always advocated how brilliant a platform it was. Because she had been so vocal about her presence on OnlyFans, and *Packed Lunch* were seemingly still happy to use her as a co-presenter from time to time, I assumed neither the show nor Channel 4 would have an issue with me being on there, too. I did still wonder if I could reasonably align my role as a daytime television personality with the use of such a subscription service, but because of Kerry's on-screen time, I assumed – ignorantly, I guess – that I could.

I had also become increasingly aware that, because of *Strictly*, I had many more young followers than I'd had before. I didn't feel it appropriate for my more questionable content to be easily accessed by younger eyes. Yes, I could have just nipped it in the bud altogether, but on some level, I was – and still am – proud of the hard work I had invested in my physical health and fitness; though, it could, and should, have been celebrated privately, just for myself.

Of course, the financial potential of using OnlyFans was also alluring. It seemed that the small investments I'd made in the form of gym sessions and careful meal-planning had a value, and OnlyFans offered dividends. Most of us are worried about paying off our mortgage and life after retirement. This was just a different way of getting there.

What I longed for most, though, was control. After ten years of working in television and publishing, I had received so many knocks (as anyone in the industry does): cancelled brand partnerships; pilots that never got the commission; morning TV shows cutting my job suddenly, just as I'd bought a new house. Just before I got on the plane to France for that holiday, my agent told me a TV show we were hoping for had been cancelled, and that *Packed Lunch* wanted to cut my days. I'm not asking for sympathy here – that's all part and parcel of a media career; every single person in this great machine will be able to share similar experiences. But I have always craved security. Even when I was a little lad in primary school, I would frequently share with Mum how panicked I was that I would never get on the housing ladder. OnlyFans offered the chance to be in control of something: no agent fees, no feeling of being used, no one to rub up the wrong way.

★ ★ ★

So there I was, bronzed and boozy in Nice, carefree and far-removed from the reality of my life and my responsibilities. I managed to convinced Paul that it would be a good thing – I could empower myself, keep my main social media cleaner and more professional, and all the while bring home some serious bacon. He was still reserved about it, but it wasn't his decision and he would never try to control mine.

I drafted an explanation for Instagram, created an OnlyFans account and waited for it to be verified. I remember receiving the email to say my account was valid and good to go. We were at the Nick Knight flower exhibition at the photography museum in Nice. As the email came through, I gazed at the photographs before me. I considered the experience Nick Knight had garnered from years of hard graft and building relationships. I instantly felt cheap and easy. I tried to remind myself of the years of hard work I had put in at the gym, but it didn't completely work. At the back of my mind, I knew there was nothing talented about me taking a photograph of my bare arse and sharing it with the world.

Integrity is a strange thing. We often judge one another and question each other's integrity. We think integrity is balancing our decisions and choices with the average notion of what is universally considered to be right and proper, but is that really the case? Is it more often about balancing the position we are in at the time with what we consider aligns with our own moral sense? It's the perfect example of what it is to be an adult: making tough decisions for ourselves, regardless of the opinions of others. I tried to reason with myself in this way, too: this is what *I* want and I should feel proud about it.

Before I could reason with myself any more, the money started to roll in. Within a few hours of using the site, I'd made thousands. Even Paul's jaw hit the floor when I showed him. And I wasn't showing anything too obscene; 'No pole, no hole' was the rule I made for myself. Just pictures of me in my swimwear, me in my gym wear and my buttocks, though I did cave in to requests for tasteful nudes on a couple of occasions.

What I didn't anticipate was just how bloody funny it would become. I'd writhe around on the bed, trying to get the right angle to make everything look top-notch and impossibly pert.

Paul would ask me to hold a position as he took the photographs, and my bad back would flare up, so I'd grimace unflatteringly as he snapped me from behind. He, being the artist he is, would scout a position as I lay naturally on the beach, and he'd instruct me to hold it. As soon as the lens fell upon me, though, it'd look completely strained, like a ruddy unruly toddler forcing out a fart. If anything, it made us laugh, which we really needed to do together after a tough year.

Then there were the requests from my 'fans', which I'd never anticipated. One man (I'm assuming it was a man, though I do know for a fact that some women also signed up) asked me to take a video of myself smoking a Marlboro Light cigarette, wearing a leather jacket, while I ate a packet of Walker's salt and vinegar crisps. I mean, I'm all for the joyous fetish of junk food from time to time, but that was an invitation I just couldn't get my head around. I was offered £1,000 for it, but I declined. That was something way beyond my boundaries. Probably for the best; I much prefer a Pringle.

Then there was the 'judicial feeder', as I affectionately named him. An anonymous judge offered to pay me £500 a month to begin a serious weight bulk, and for every half stone I gained, he would pay me a bonus of an extra £500. I wondered how tight the contract would be, considering we both had legal backgrounds. Should I instruct independent legal advice to draft it, or would he ensure it was bilaterally beneficial? Would my weigh-in be on the scales of justice?

I received countless requests for feet pictures, numerous offers for my used underwear – these things really were a far cry from the cheeky snaps I'd moved over from Instagram. But there was something so empowering about it. That's a thing many OnlyFans content creators have noted: how empowering it is. And you'd be forgiven if you instantly assumed that it was the validation and fawning that was emboldening, but that's not it at all. It was the ability to say 'no' that I found so fulfilling. I was able to enforce my boundaries in a kind, non-judgemental way – I mean, hey, we've all got our kinks, so who was I to belittle someone for making a polite request? If someone asked for something I wasn't willing to give, I'd firmly but politely decline. That was a notion I had struggled with all my life. I've never liked to upset people, so often gave too much of myself away.

Being in control of my own ship on OnlyFans quite quickly percolated into everyday life. When you work in television, it's so easy to be a 'yes person'. Through fear of being dropped, there's a tendency to agree to everything: yes, I'll drop a day off with my boyfriend to cover for someone; yes, I'll fail to attend a friend's wedding or family funeral to shoot some random pilot about bread. What I found, though, was that I valued the power of saying 'no' more. Not in an arbitrary or unkind way, but if something didn't fit in with my plans or sense of integrity, I was more than happy to say, 'Thank you, but no thank you.' Who'd have thought such an important life lesson would come from rejecting an offer to munch on a packet of crisps with a fag in my hand?

When I landed back in England, the *Sun* had already written

an article about my move to OnlyFans. I posted the explanation
I'd drafted on Instagram and my agent rang me. We'd worked
together for ten years, and one of the first things he said to
me that day was, 'You're John Whaite; you have always done
what you want.' He wasn't mad; he was kind. He's one of
the few people who have seen every facet of my character, so he
wasn't totally surprised that in an impulsive moment, after a few
bits of bad news, I'd lurched in another direction. But he was
naturally concerned about my job in mainstream TV. The editor
of *Packed Lunch* had already called him to ask what on earth was
going on. He, too, wasn't angry, just concerned.

It made the usual comedown after a holiday a thousand times
worse. I panicked that I'd be instantly dropped from *Packed Lunch*
and Channel 4, from my contract as a chef for the Waitrose online
channels and all the other working relationships I had carefully
nurtured over the years. Steph McGovern texted me to say,
'You've made a lot of press today.' She reminded me that while
my intentions in using OnlyFans were pure, you cannot change
the preconceptions of other people.

It's a tricky one, that, isn't it? The majority of my Instagram
followers praised my decision to move some content over to
OnlyFans. They understood my reasoning and appreciated my
honesty. But they were only a small percentage of my audience.
My agent reminded me that I wasn't just 'John from Wigan'
any more, and that eyes from all over the world and different
industries were on me. There was no immediate fallout from the

move I had made, but I could feel an undercurrent of questioning and judgement from many.

That made me further question the idea of integrity. Because while I'd convinced myself that integrity is personal, and can only be judged internally and uniquely, I'd failed to remember we don't thrash around in the vacuum of our own existence. As painful or difficult as it sometimes is, our choices are – and have to be – made with a consideration of what society at large considers to be reasonable. And this doesn't mean being sycophantic or forcibly yielding; it's just that we cannot be our own boss, customer, spiritual coach, parent, friend or ally, all at the same time. Society pivots on people and the merging of ideas, and with that, individual, stand-alone integrity is diluted.

That hit me hard, and shame creeped its way in. Shame is such an insidious emotion. It's loud and obnoxious, yet so discreet at the same time. Whenever I posted a picture, I'd feel a little bit dirty. I allowed the judgement of others to get to me – the raised eyebrows became my morality checks. I could tell my mum hated it. She tried to be impartial, to let me take responsibility for my own actions, but I could see in her eyes how much she disapproved. She'd frequently ask me whether I was doing hardcore porn. I asked her whether it would be so terrible if I were, and made it clear that my view of sex work was that it should be respected and regulated, like any other industry. She said she shared this notion, but what she worried about was how I could align my daytime TV role with a platform that is known mostly for empowering sex workers. If I gave up TV and became a porn star, she wouldn't care, as long as I was happy. She was just concerned about the opinions of others becoming so detrimental that they might destroy the career I loved and had worked hard for.

I knew that was a possibility, but I tried hard to talk myself out of that mindset. I told myself that the media industry is heavily sexualised anyway, and that ever since I had got more muscular in my frame, I seemed to be more in demand for television work. I also considered the fact that Luke Kempner had joked about me being on OnlyFans on *Steph's Packed Lunch* – jokes that had, of course, been signed off by the day producer and editor. So could they or the channel still really have concerns about my online presence? As I sat watching *Naked Attraction*, the Channel 4 show in which people get completely nude, I felt that maybe the world was simply becoming more overt.

People did begin to change towards me, though. Some distanced themselves, and it upset me greatly. I felt they gave more consideration to the headline 'John Whaite joins adult site OnlyFans' than to the truth of me as a person. Paradoxically, I guess, that's a danger of the world of social media: I wanted to reap the benefits of such a platform, of selling a façade of myself, but I still expected people to see through it, to automatically understand my entire decision-making process with all the nuance. But it doesn't work like that. We don't naturally walk a mile in a man's shoes before we judge him; we simply question his footwear choice and leave it at that.

★ ★ ★

I knew I needed to put an end to it, but I felt trapped. Of course, the money I was making had an appeal and was a huge incentive to remain on the platform. But on top of that, I felt a responsibility to those fans who had paid for subscriptions: a responsibility to deliver the goods for a reasonable amount of time. I also stubbornly wanted to prove that I had no shame in exposing a side of myself that was more body-positive and open-minded – but I was kidding myself in that regard, because shame overtook a lot of my thinking. What I didn't realise was that I was crossing my own boundary; a boundary that I had never previously met. I didn't, and don't, judge others for using sites like OnlyFans and so assumed I too would feel comfortable doing so.

The question of integrity became even more vital when a news article suggested that child exploitation was still happening on OnlyFans. It was possible, the journalist claimed, for child pornography to be shared on the site. As soon as I read this, I had to remove myself from the platform. I couldn't comfortably profit from a sexualised façade of myself if the fetishisation of minors was occurring just a few doors down. I immediately started the deactivation process and also deleted my Whaite Lifter Instagram account. Instantly, I felt a weight lifted.

My two months on OnlyFans taught me a great deal. The process solidified the fact that, as individuals, we can't expect other people to fully understand the complexity of a situation. They are bound to judge it at face value. We can't hold that against them. Those who want to listen, will, and those who don't, won't. Our actions have consequences regardless of the reasoning behind them, because the actions are all that are seen at first glance. It is the actions, after all, that carry the weight, the impact.

What I've been so grateful to learn is that the weight that I give to everyone else's opinion has, until now, been universal and equal. No matter the person nor the role they played in my life, I would consider their opinions as gospel, which served only to dilute my own sense of integrity. Part of integrity is distinguishing the people we trust the most from the people we trust the least – who we align with, why and what they have to say. Some raised eyebrows are judgement, while others are from a place of concern and love. It's on us – it was on me – to learn the difference.

And I realised, most importantly of all, that integrity is not a solid, unmalleable block of concrete. It's a haunting and mysterious shapeshifter, elusive until it's truly called into question. But when it is, it can reveal itself with a punch to the gut. When that happens, we have a choice: shame spiral or learn.

10.
There's Work to Be Done

———

In the year after *Strictly*, I saw Johannes less. We spoke every now and again, but as wild horses do, he danced away into the dust and carried on with his fabulous life. I knew I had to let him go. Not just for my own sake, not even just for Paul's, but for his, too. Members of the public would prophesy, 'You boys will be friends for life!', and in some way they are right. I hope to always have contact with him, to hear his joyful laugh that is both high-pitched and deeply booming at the same time. I'll never forget the blend of South African slang and English that he'd sometimes default to – his *Johannerisms*, as I called them. I had not a bloody clue what the hell he was on about half the time, but I could get the gist of it from the tone of his voice and his eyerolls. He'll forever be my partner in changing the course of history, and nothing could take that away from us. His name will be etched on my heart until it takes its final beat. Love doesn't just stop because you want it to. But that was a love that was incubated by the limelight and grew in swanky hotels and on the stages of arenas across the country. Paul would live with me on the streets if it came to that.

Finding my way out of the *Strictly* maelstrom was a simpler feat. It just happened. Suddenly. Steph McGovern and I went to watch the cast of 2022 in the Blackpool Tower Ballroom. We sat in the audience seats, too close together and crammed in, sipping from the contraband hipflask of rum that I had smuggled in in my underpants. I'd felt nervous about going, about feeling like the bus had left the station without me on it. But as I sat wide-eyed in this beautiful, ornate ballroom, with both the scattering lights and the intricate coral-like carvings plunging me forty fathoms below, I had a realisation: *it's all a spectacle. It isn't real.* The only thing between this and my first production of *Snow White* at Chorley Little Theatre back in 1993 was budget and production value. Sure, the audience applause from *Strictly* was so loud that it made the Earth shake. But an audience won't kiss you goodnight or hold you tight when you're sobbing uncontrollably. External validation won't look into your eyes and hold your hand as you take your final breath. Only the people who love you can do that. I wasn't still clinging on to my magic mirror from thirty years before, so I needed to let the mirrorball roll away, too. And I did. There and then. But the hard work had only just begun.

★ ★ ★

I woke up shivering on the carpet, with a light blanket covering me, my shoulders exposed and cold. I thought to myself, my sister must have woken up in the night, found me on the floor and covered me up. I didn't open my eyes, but I could sense the light, diffused pink through my eyelids. I was aware of that strange sound of nothing transitioning to the gentle murmur of the morning. I was sure that soon enough, Mum would start to stir in the kitchen and the ghost of toast would creep its way up the stairs. My sister would probably step over me any minute now, sighing, put out that I was plonked in front of her door as I always was.

I'm seeing Dad today! I thought to myself. But I couldn't remember what for. I couldn't figure out why, when normally I'd be so excited to see him, today there was a subtle shaking in the pit of my stomach – an anxiety that made me want to tell the sun that the moon gave us enough light, to ask the songbirds to take the morning off.

I started to latch on to a scent, but it wasn't the nutty bitterness of bread turning from white to golden. It was stronger, more pungent – acrid almost. It was a recognisable smell, but not one of comfort. I opened one eye, straining, as the light burned too bright. Nausea kicked in, and my head throbbed. I quickly realised what that smell was, as the bowl of vomit shifted into focus. My sisters weren't here, and Mum wasn't in the kitchen. Abel ran into the bedroom and brushed past me to clamber under the bed where he usually lies with all his toys – his babies – growling if anyone gets too close to his collection of eviscerated stuffed pheasants and bunny rabbits with their eyes torn off.

It was Christmas Day 2022, and I was beyond hungover. The afternoon before I'd popped out to a friend's party, vowing only to have one glass of wine. I'd spent the week drinking quite heavily, so wanted to be a bit gentler with myself. I'd also promised to help Mum in the kitchen the next day, and I *really* didn't want to let her down. While she'd wanted to throw a buffet – something a bit easier after losing the full use of her right arm in an horrific accident a few years prior – she'd somehow decided that we should have a proper dinner – big table, seating plan, the usual. Mum had spent the week preparing, peeling vegetables and polishing the cutlery, while my stepdad helped trim the house and get the table ready. Ibsam, the wooden stag's head in their oak-framed dining room, had his feather boa and Santa hat on, and I'd made a spread of desserts – sticky toffee pudding and pavlova, as always.

At the party on Christmas Eve, a floppy-hatted little elf had wandered around, pouring champagne for us all, keeping my glass full. Flashbacks poured into my mind of a real donkey being paraded through the kitchen, the handler with a tea towel on his head dressed as Joseph. I remembered rattling around the garden on a mobility scooter, balancing my champagne flute between my legs as I tore across the gravel. At one point, I had wobbled on someone's shoulders – maybe Paul's, but I don't think it would have been his – as I tried to etch an apostrophe into the house sign that was missing one. I'd let myself get so drunk that as Paul drove us home to feed the dog, I made him stop the car to let me out at the pub, where I continued to throw back the booze. Once he'd sorted out our responsibilities back at the house, he came to find me, propped up against the bar, surrounded by empty sambuca glasses, swaying as I asked people at the bar if they feared death.

This wasn't unusual. Not since the aftermath of *Bake Off*. I'd relied increasingly on alcohol to lighten the mood for a long time. But it had become more than a mood-enhancer, it had become the destination at the end of every long week – sometimes the end of every long day. My ability to have one glass and one alone is mythical. Family parties would become excuses for getting drunk, and I'd look forward to social events not solely because I wanted to catch up with my closest friends, but because they'd be an opportunity to get inebriated. I needed to feel something, the power of something greater than myself. There were often times during therapy when I told my counsellor I wanted to go to church. But the only altar I returned to was that of destruction, with my holy wine glass overflowing.

Although it's true to say that most of the time I wasn't aware that my drinking was an issue, I did make occasional attempts to address it, but this generally involved nothing more than trite morning-after declarations of sobriety, which would usually be shredded and pulped in a goblet of Cab Sauv by the end of the very same day. Although not a daily drinker (five days out of seven, perhaps), I have to hold myself accountable and admit that I am problematic drinker. I'd need a few extra limbs to be able to count on my fingers all the times one drink had turned into a binge, during which I'd stay up all night, drinking alone in the front room. Messaging strangers on social media just to have someone to talk to. I won't say how much I drank – not to be cryptic or secretive, but just because I don't think it's useful. If you read these words and have a feeling you need to rein in your alcohol consumption, then do. It isn't helpful to compare yourself to another person, because that can easily become the reason not to stop: *oh he drank more than me, I'm fine.* I don't know if I'd class myself as an alcoholic, but I'm certainly an addictive person.

Looking back, it was during my time on the farm in Canada that a seed was planted that would take five years to germinate. I witnessed there how emotionally volatile alcohol makes me. After just one afternoon at the Barriere Motor Inn drinking a few pints, I woke up feeling like a different person. Weeks of a peaceful mindset and mental imperviousness to day-to-day problems were instantly replaced with feeling more paranoid, more impatient, and needing more junk food. It made me feel so closed off, when before I'd been so open to the beautiful surroundings. I had spent moments awestruck by the spikes of hoar frost on wire fences; the patter of snowflakes as they fell to the ground; the lick of the calf's sandpaper tongue against my forehead as I shattered the ice on her water trough. Now I focused on myself, my feelings, my needs. Alcohol shifted my attention from the outside to the inside, and not in the necessary and curative way of introspection, but rather as an overbearing symptom of negativity. Alcohol makes emotion drive you. Sobriety, on the other hand, invites reason to guide you.

★ ★ ★

The night before my university graduation, I went to dinner with the girls I had spent most of my law course with. We got dressed up, rightly proud of ourselves and the years of work we had each put into our achievements. We had food with a few rounds of drinks, but in anticipation of the big day to come, they all set off home. I, on the other hand, went out. Alone. I got drunk, chatted shit with strangers, then woke up on the couch at 4am to Paul wafting smoke from beneath the screeching fire alarm – I'd left a Dr. Oetker Ristorante Pizza in the oven, and it was totally incinerated, filling the apartment with smoke.

My graduation the next day was hell. I nursed a hangover and rode the never-ending waves of nausea, while trying to smile for photos and throwing my mortarboard sky high. I went for dinner, during which I was impatient and rude, and fell out with my mum. I just wanted to sleep and eat a Domino's pizza. My behaviour the night before had ruined what ought to have been one of the proudest moments of my life. I didn't have the self-respect to say, 'I'm going to go home, have a bath and get a good rest for tomorrow's important and much-deserved celebration.'

Whenever I taught a class in my cookery school, after twelve hours on my feet, half of which were spent entertaining ten strangers, I would be knackered. What I should have done was go home, sleep, recuperate. Instead, I'd get so drunk with some of my students that after they'd gone home and I had cleaned the kitchen, Paul and I would head straight to the pub, which would turn into a train journey into Manchester and an all-nighter there. The next week would then be a mountain climb – totally ruined by a hangover – so when I finally reached the summit, I'd want to celebrate and let off steam with another round of drinks.

Alcohol, for many of us and most definitely for me, is a shield. It acts as a coping strategy. I used it to help me handle both the shit life flings at me and the painful pangs of the past. Rather than me having to deal with unprocessed memories, alcohol acted as barrier. However, I've come to learn that it's a shield that can ultimately prove to be too heavy for the carrier and can end up crushing them under its mighty weight.

★ ★ ★

That Christmas Day, after I'd woken up on the floor, was a challenge. I'd invited Dad round for breakfast. I wanted to cancel, to sleep it off, to eat junk. But I couldn't do that to Dad. He was nearly eighty, and I didn't see him anywhere near enough. I took a shower to wash off the stench and the shame, and looked at my face in the mirror. That freckle under my eye was still there. It had faded a little, obscured by a wrinkle, but those were still the eyes of the little lad who used to stare back at me; the boy who fought through the fear of the farmhouse; the teenager who may not have had the courage or vocabulary to speak his truth, but who performed it loudly while dyeing his hair and dancing with the girls.

I made Welsh rarebit and fried eggs, served champagne and orange juice – I just had the orange juice – and ploughed through the conversation, doing my best to keep myself from throwing up.

That night, at Mum's house, it all came crashing down. There was a situation during the cooking – nothing noteworthy – that led to a little tension between Mum, my sisters and me. Had I not been hungover, I could have dealt with it more effectively and kindly. Instead, I was impatient and curt, unkind in some of the things I said. I wasn't solely to blame for the situation, but I was entirely to blame for my actions. I stood there in my beautiful sequinned bomber jacket, reeling ugly and spiteful incantations intended to invoke pain. Mum was so upset she wanted me to leave. On Christmas Day. I vowed never to drink again after that, but just three days later, I found myself up all night in Manchester, dancing and drinking everything in sight. My last drink was a bloody Mary, locked in an underground bar talking to a handful of other lost souls who didn't want to face the dawn.

What I realised the next morning, as I sobbed in Paul's arms, is that I felt nihilistic and embittered again. I felt suicidal. I found a picture of me and Mum in my drawer from when I was a baby. I could see how much she loved me in the photograph, how proud she seemed to be clutching this bundle of joy. And I thought about how disappointed she was in me now. In that moment, I knew I had one option: sobriety. Yes, I'd made that false promise to myself a thousand times. I'd even tried to go a few weeks without drinking, but had always fallen off the wagon. But there was something different this time. It was as though all the times I'd well and truly caused chaos replayed in my mind, with the strong stench of booze pervading everything. It hadn't been enough, in the past, to just *want* to stop drinking. That had always failed. This time, I needed to reconfigure my mindset and ask myself *why* I wanted to stop drinking. Adding that link, that 'because', became the reason. To improve relationships with the people I love. To cut out relationships that are toxic or damaging. To stop gaslighting myself or eroding my self-esteem. To save money – a lot of money. To look after my mental wellbeing. To look after my physical wellbeing. To confront the facts of my past and not the fantasy.

Over the first few weeks of my sobriety, Our Vic checked in with me regularly. Whenever I fancied a cold beer after work, or a glass of Aran Sherry Cask in bed, she'd remind me that the years of hard work she had put into her abstinence – which was, by this time, coming close to four – could all be unravelled with a single drop. She was so right. One glass of whisky in bed is fine, but it opens the floodgates to me drinking again; if I can have a whisky in bed on a Tuesday night, then I can have a bottle of wine, or two, on a Friday, Saturday and Sunday. And if I've polished off a bottle of wine, I may as well go clubbing to celebrate a week of hard work. And if I'm out clubbing, well, I may as well stay out until the first train home.

No, John. Grow up.

She sent me titles of books to read, links to inspirational people on social media who I could look up to. She had gathered a toolkit for her own survival and shared it with me, her little brother. Like her, I got back into exercise for the *right* reasons. I focused not on my size or shape, on self-flagellation for aesthetics, but on the struggle itself. As I pedalled on my spin bike, I concentrated on the push and pull of my legs, just as I'd paid attention to my steps while walking the West Highland Way. I tried to make every physical thing I performed into a meditation, to stay disciplined. I tried to find peace in the mundane, like I had in Canada. The day-to-day tasks we perform, from making the bed in the morning to drying the pots at night, are not obligations;

they are merely patterns that we ourselves create to keep us from going insane.

I reflected on my failures, too. Of course, I needed help; that's undeniable. But I can't be too gentle on myself. Yes, we have to love ourselves and forgive ourselves, but I think a fundamental part of self-love is holding yourself accountable. It's not about just forgiving yourself for your mistakes without any reflection on how much damage they've caused; it's about earning that forgiveness for yourself. Self-love isn't a bubble bath and an expensive candle. It is gruelling, painful work. It's about slapping yourself on the wrist when you're being destructive, when you're rolling through life like a boulder, flattening everything in your path.

The damage I caused to my relationship with Paul was a huge catalyst in this change. Mum always told me, 'You can't have bits of people; you either accept them fully and for who they are, or you don't accept them at all.' But I disagree with that sentiment. I now see that you can't *have* people full stop. Love with ultimatums or judgement just isn't love. If we are lucky, we get to exist alongside another person, growing together, sometimes getting tangled in each other's branches, but still standing alone. It was a miracle that Paul had put up with me over the years. Not just for what happened after *Strictly*, but as a frightened kitten I often scratched viciously with my emotions. I've been needy and jealous. But he gave me the space to figure that out for myself, to grow. I've been a patch of soil that he has nurtured, fed and watered as time has ticked away. He hasn't tried to manicure or perfect me, but rather has stood patiently at the gate, waiting for me to grow into whatever I am destined to be, shouting words of encouragement from time to time, accepting the weeds among the flowers. I've never felt love quite like it. A love that has evolved from ownership and obsession to a healthy self-possession that acknowledges distance and individuality not as great chasms, but as necessary moments of repose and reconfiguration.

It is, in fact, difficult to reduce the relationship I share with Paul to a few thousand words across the pages of a book, because it transcends grammar and vocabulary. When the fizz and sparkle of our lives has faded, and we are reduced to nothing but mere memory and the dash between two dates on a headstone, none of those things – words, memories or dates – could ever be enough to illustrate the bond we have shared. While we may merely be two temporary pinpricks on this spinning globe, what we have is an entire universe of our own: intangible and sacred, evolving and eternal. It is built on trust – which itself is born of a mutual learning from mistakes made and experiences had. It is about making small sacrifices for one another, while learning to be true to ourselves. The story is worthy of Greek myth; the players are undeniably human, but the bond itself, that magic glue, is divine.

★ ★ ★

I've found spending more time with the other people I love to be helpful in fighting off the urge to forget the past and predict the future. I watch my nephews as they dig muddy trenches in Mum's back garden and fish in the stream down in the woods, their cheeks red as they laugh and swear and push boundaries. I sit with the emotion it brings to witness their growth. Joy, yes, but a little sadness for the horrors they will inevitably stumble across as they evolve. I hope they won't grow up like I did, trying to temper their identity and behaviour just to please the world, performing a delicate dance. But the reality is, it is the often the world that tells the child who they should be, before they're given the grace to figure it all out for themselves.

But there's some reassurance in the knowledge that as the Earth turns, our identities don't just get lost and linger on the dark side, hidden from the sun. We can shed the skins that no longer serve a purpose. For so long I tried to figure out what box I should tick, how to describe myself in a tidy soundbite to please other men, an audience, producers and commissioners. What's true is that who I am meant to be, where I am supposed to be in the timeline of my life, will fall into place if I just chomp down on the bit and work hard. While fear is a great driver of output and should even be welcomed to the party sometimes, it is a guest that should be treated with great caution – like the kleptomaniac aunt who always tries to pilfer the pepper shaker. We are always going to compare ourselves to others; I guess that is a part of what it means to be human. But that comparison should be used to derive advice and tricks with which to arm ourselves for our own experiences and goals. We should use it as guidance to help us jump the hurdles that are directly in our path, rather than those over which others have long since leapt. We strive to have something that is so regimented and perfect sometimes that we fail to see the beauty in the rugged and natural. I've come to learn that a wild meadow is far more beautiful than a manicured lawn.

And just as *my* identity isn't set in stone, neither is that of anyone else. My mum isn't just my mum. She is a sister, a granny, a wife, a daughter, a friend, a businesswoman, a frightened child, a flawed human. She is a million different things to a million different people, and for me to hold her in one single light isn't kind or empathetic. The same is true of my dad, my stepdad and of all the fellow scrambles of atoms on this marbled ball with whom I share my existence. None of the people I looked up to, or glared at angrily for what I considered to be their failures, have had some divine blueprint to follow. They've had their hearts broken and they themselves have broken hearts. They too navigate the question of what it is to be human on a daily basis. It's possible to hold people accountable without dehumanising them.

★ ★ ★

It's the morning after the Fortnum and Mason awards 2023 I'm almost 140 days sober. Last night was a really lovely event, but at about 8.30pm I'd had enough and walked alone back to my hotel, proud of not even feeling an urge to drink alcohol – another victory to celebrate. Quietly. Just for myself. I chatted to industry friends, spoke proudly in my deep, northern voice about the bits and bobs I was up to in work, without embellishment or exaggeration. Then I quietly slipped away, putting one grey suede boot before the other, trusting them to carry me to my bed. Paul's coming down to London to meet me today. We'll probably have dinner and see friends. It's *unlikely* that we'll end up licking a pole in some sticky-floored gay nightclub at 5am, though, never say never. I won't take a hostage to fortune.

I'm still dancing on eggshells; we all are, because that is what it is to be human. But they seem to be no longer tossed together with the fragments of my own guilt and shame, or the mistaken view that those who love me loathed me. These sharp little shards may still represent the judgement and prejudices of others, but these days it feels liberating to hear them crunch beneath my feet as I spin and twirl. I hope they turn to dust and scatter in the wind. Now, on to the next chapter, hey?

Acknowledgements

Writing this memoir has been a beautiful thing – not just because it's given me the luxury of looking back over my life, taking stock and analysing it – but also, because of the interaction with different people it has afforded me.

I firstly must thank Paul, my Peebs. You've given me so much time, love, forgiveness and understanding. If the world were full of more people like you, it would turn that bit more beautifully.

Jonny, my friend, thank you for believing in me, and counselling me through the dark moments of doubt that shrouded this process – I love you man.

Judith, I appreciate you. Your patience, compassion and care have been so important. Jo, thank you for the title idea. Mel, the cover is perfect – thank you for blocking out the noise and creating something so perfectly personal. Emma, thank you for your care and attention to detail. Everyone at Kyle Books – cheers. Tara, thank you for doing such a forensic and mindful job with the editing. Dean and Martin – what a cover photo!

Theia, Anna and the KBJ gang – thank you so much for everything, you gals rock!

My friends – the Bolton lot and the Mawdsley clan, and the posh southern lot – I love you guys. Thank you for being there over the years through thick and thin, for accepting me for all that I am. Lucy B, you're an angel creature – we are lucky to have you in our lives – thank you for your time and compassion. Katie B – thank you for giving me the workspace to write this.

Kate Quilton, thanks for listening to my rants and worries throughout our South Korea trip, and for being cover consultant extraordinaire. Concepta, thank you for being ever present and ever willing to give your time and wisdom. Tim, thank you for your thoughtful feedback at the 11th hour.

To Steph, Vivek, Matt and the gang at *Steph's Packed Lunch*, and Jo and Jayne and the rest of Channel 4 – thanks for renewing my love of TV, and for giving me a second chance. Courtney, my Maura, I love you, but where the f**k are Mum's tiny ceramic shoes? Sarah, thanks for keeping us unruly kids in line, and for being so calm and gorgeous. Leigh (and Amanda) – I don't know how I'll ever be able to repay you for your kindness.

Russell T. Davies – I'm honoured (and still in disbelief) that you'd even want to read my manuscript, let alone share the most beautiful words about it. Thank you so very much – not just for the words, but for paving the way, making the world a better place with all the work you do to represent our community.

To my family – I love you all so much. I'm proud to be a part of our tribe, and I'm so grateful to you all for forgiving all of my messes.

Mum, I love you with every ounce of my being, and you never have to doubt that. Thank you for your guidance, your love, your protection, your vulnerability and your strength. And of course I still love nipping to Lilian Harrison's with you – I'll never be too old for a supermarket trip with mama.